MW01249159

FORT MCINTOSH AND THE PARANORMAL

CHRIS JAMES

i

DEDICATION

This book is dedicated to Sofia Juarez, the future of ghost hunting. She showed up every night all Throughout October to attended ghost hunts at Laredo College, and she brought her own equipment.

Cover and inside drawings by
Leticia Reyes
Former Laredo Community College Art Student
And sister-in-law of Chris James

ACKNOWLEDGMENTS

I did a lot of research while writing this book. I spent many days sitting in libraries while librarians and clerks pulled books from shelves and piled them in front of me.
Thanks to all of you.

Renee Laperier, Librarian II, Laredo Public Library
Dr. Ricardo J. Solis, President of Laredo College
Jackie Longoria, Circulation Assistant
Abrahan Garza, Periodicals Clerk
Rosa Rios, Circulation Supervisor
Dr. Rodney Rodriguez, Executive Director of Strategic & External Initiatives
Carmelino Castillo Jr. Director of Student Life
Raquel A. Peña, Associate Dean of Students
Rita Canales, and Annette Hekking, at the Border Patrol Museum
Christina Villarreal and Margarita Araiza with the Webb Co. Heritage Foundation

Chris James

1 CAMP CRAWFORD

Laredo or Villa de San Agustin de Laredo as it was first named, was founded in 1755 and was located on the Rio Grande River near a low water crossing. El Paseo de Jacinto was used to cross the river as long as weather was good and there were no rains to the north which would raise the river to a dangerous level.

Tomás Sánchez de la Barrera had been a captain in the Spanish Army and was sent by the king of Spain to build a settlement that would support the crossing. The small village was named after Laredo, Cantabria, Spain which is located on the coast of Northern Spain in the area known as Basque Country.

With the signing of the Treaty of Cordoba on August 24, 1821, Mexico gained their independence from Spain. Antonio de Padua María Severino López de Santa Anna y Pérez de Lebrón better known simply as Santa Ana had begun his career as an infantry officer in the Spanish army. When it looked as if Mexico might just win Santa Ana switched his allegiance and joined the rebellion.

Mexico named the northern part of Mexico the state of Coahuila y Tejas.

Santa Anna was elected president of Mexico on April 1, 1833. In 1835, Santa Anna repealed the Mexican Constitution, which ultimately led to the beginning of the Texas Revolution.

In 1836, Texas became its own republic claiming land from the Red River to the Rio Grande. Mexico decided the border was the Nueces River since they called the Rio Grande the Rio

Bravo. To Mexico, the Rio Grande was the Nueces River. This lead to a huge area of land that was disputed by both countries.

In 1838 Texas President Mirabeau B. Lamar raised a force of 56 Rangers to run the Mexican military out of the southern portion of Texas and fight the Cherokee and the Comanche raiding parties that were preying on small settlements.

Santa Ana had decided he wanted to reclaim the lands lost to Texas. He began making, what looked like, preparations to invade the country to the north.

President Lamar thought it would be a good idea to have a country between them and Mexico so he convinced people living in North Mexico to secede from their home country as well. Coahuila, Nuevo Leon, and Tamaulipas all joined together to form the Republic of the Rio Grande. The republic's capital was placed in Laredo to put it as far from Mexico City as possible.

This new country only lasted from January 17 to November 6, 1840. A lot of brave men were sacrificed trying to create a country.

The Republic of Texas was strapped for cash. They had no way of raising money to pay for any of the things a country was expected to provide. The folks living along the Rio Grande as well as the western parts of the country were being plagued by bandit raids as well as Indian attacks. The idea was being discussed amongst the citizens that it would be beneficial for the Republic to become a state. On December 29, 1845, Congress admitted Texas to the U.S. as a constituent state of the Union.

Mexico still considered the lands south of the Nueces River to belong to them. The United States considered this land to belong to the State of Texas and therefore a part of the U.S. and this lead to the Mexican-American War which began in 1846.

Antonio López de Santa Anna, or simply Santa Ana, wrote a letter to Mexico City stating he did not care to return to the presidency but would like to come out of exile in Cuba, due to his last presidency he had been thrown out of Mexico. He offered to use his military experience to reclaim Texas for Mexico.

Hiram Ulises Grant, better known as Ulises S Grant, was a lieutenant assigned as the Regimental Quartermaster. He managed to lead a cavalry charge at the Battle of Resaca de la Palma and rode as a dispatch rider at the Battle of Monterrey.

Robert E Lee was a Captain in the U.S. Army during the Mexican–American War. Lee was instrumental in several American victories by personally reconnoitering routes of attack that the Mexicans had not defended thinking the terrain was impassable.

Lee was promoted to Brevet Colonel. Brevet means you hold the rank only temporarily and don't get the pay. At the end of the war in 1848 Colonel Lee was returned to the rank of captain.

William Tecumseh Sherman was a lieutenant serving on the western edge of the war. He never saw any combat.

James Longstreet served with General Scott during the Mexican-American War. He was a lieutenant but earned two brevet promotions, ending the conflict as a brevet Major. He also returned to the rank of Lieutenant at wars end.

Thomas "Stonewall" Jackson was a Lieutenant during the war. Jackson's unit came under heavy fire and as his men all ran for cover Jackson drug a small cannon onto the road and began singlehandedly firing at the enemy. He was soon joined by a few more men and a second cannon and they fought a raging battle against the Mexican gunmen and artillery.

Lieutenant George McClellan, Pierre Gustave Toutant

Beauregard, Ambrose Burnside, Braxton Bragg, and George Meade, all served in the United States Army during the 1846 to 1848 war. All of these men would fight on either side of the American Civil War. Half for the Union and half for the CSA.

Colonel Jefferson Davis, later President of the Confederate States, raised a volunteer regiment, named the 1st Mississippi Rifles. At the time most units were still using smooth bore muzzle loading muskets. The rifles were a far superior weapon. There accuracy made the rifles a deadly weapon at longer ranges.

In 1846, after the Battle of Monterrey, Texas Governor Henderson wanted to send troupes to Laredo to protect this isolated town. General Taylor didn't think this was a good idea since Laredo was of no military value as far as he was concerned.

Mirabeau Buonaparte Lamar, former President of the Republic of Texas and now serving as Inspector General, resigned his position and was commissioned as Captain of Volunteers. Eighty Texas Rangers reenlisted as United States Troupes under Lamar. This unit was sent to defend Laredo against any Mexican invasion. The troupes were also used to track down bandits and stop Indian raids on the ranches around the area.

There was no military post in Laredo so the troupes were housed in and around the main plaza. The population at the time was 1,900 people which included West Laredo which was on the Mexico side of the Rio Grande.

Lamar let the Alcalde, (a Magistrate or Mayor in a Spanish town) take care of most of the legal concerns of the city. Both sides of the river continued to act like one city. When it was time for elections, folks from both sides of the river would run for office and vote for all of the positions. Only forty men showed up to vote on election day of whom thirty-seven lived in Mexico. Laredo was sitting in two countries but running as one town.

In September 1847, Lamar ordered the two towns to form separate governments and only United States Citizens could vote on the east side of the river. After this the town on the west side of the river was called Laredo de Monterrey.

The troupes in Laredo were upset at not seeing any of the "Action" of the war. It didn't help any when pay was late or non-existent.

The troupes found it impossible to do what they weren't being paid for since they had few horses. Most of the animals were being sent to the soldiers doing the actual fighting and this led to even more moral problems. Bandits or Indians would raid a ranch or small village a distance from Laredo. Word would get back to the troupes that they were needed. The only way for them to respond was on foot. By the time the troupes arrived, the fighting was over and the attackers were long gone.

People living in Laredo felt as if the United States didn't care for their wellbeing. They wrote a community letter requesting the town be turned over to Mexico. Washington was not about to hand over any town, no matter how isolated it might be, to another country. This did nothing to instill a sense of belonging to the United States. The troupes were looked on as if they were far worse than useless.

A vast majority of the countries of the world all expected Mexico to be the victor in the war. The Mexican army was larger and had experience since they had fought in many conflicts and they had the homeland advantage. What most people weren't considering was a vast majority of the Mexican troupes were conscripts who felt they only owed allegiance to their home towns and not the government in Mexico City. This led to many soldiers slipping away just before battle.

By morning, many battle plans had to be reworked to adjust for missing men. Unit commanders had little to no idea the actual strength of their companies in the field. On many occasions they discovered they were outnumbered just before marching into battle. This uncertainty began to give an advantage to the Unites States.

The U.S. troupes were just outside Mexico City preparing to attack when the Mexican politicians decided it might be a good idea to negotiate with Washington. Up until this time, the politicians all believed there was no way an invading army could get very far from the coast let alone arrive at the capital city.

The Treaty of Guadalupe Hidalgo, 1848, placed the border between the United States and Mexico as being the Rio Grande River also known as the Rio Bravo River. People living on the east side who didn't want to be United States Citizens moved to the other side of the river. Their land was then doled out to the folks still on the east side. The town known as Laredo de Monterrey became known as Nuevo Laredo. The map used to determine the location of the border had been brought from Mexico City. Once the treaty was signed it was discovered the line was off due to mistakes in the map. El Paso was still in Mexico even though it was supposed to be in the United States. The treaty had to be re-written a few times in order to get it right.

Webb County was established on January 28, 1848. Laredo was the county seat where elections would be held and most government business would take place. Laredo would be the "capital city" of the county.

In December 1848 men stationed at Camp Ringgold were ordered to march to Laredo in order to establish a military camp on the river there. This was a 120 mile march. There were no roads of any consequence. Just a trail used by merchants shipping goods to Laredo.

On March 3, 1849 Camp Crawford was established under the

command of Lt. E. L. Viele. The camp consisted of a small group of tents. The few horses were kept in corrals made by stacking brush up to create walls. The area around Laredo was lacking in any kinds of large trees to be used for wood. Not having any buildings or supplies the soldiers did their cooking and most work in the open. For things not provided by the military they had to depended on a Sutler.

A Sutler was a person who followed an army and sold provisions to the soldiers. The prices were high but this was blamed on the lack of supplies locally and the distance goods had to be shipped. Today soldiers go to the PX or Post Exchange. You can get pretty good deals on everything. A Sutler charged what they could get away with.

The troupes had some down time which was used to try to make life a bit easier for themselves. The men tried planting crops to add some fresh food their daily meals. The ground where the camp was located was unable to support growth of anything aside from mesquite and cacti. The river was just below the camp but carrying water up each and every day only turned the ground to mud. When it did rain the water would wash away anything that hadn't established deep roots.

Conditions were described as being bad, very bad. In the summer time the temperature got up to 107 degrees. There was no place to get any real shade. The few trees were small and sunlight just blazed right through the meager foliage. At night time the temperature could still run in the 90s.

Laredo only has two seasons, summer time and winter which only lasts a few weeks. A cold wind coming from the north would plow through the tents and make life miserable. The troupes all considered Camp Crawford to be the worst post in Texas, if not the entire country.

In 1850 Camp Crawford was renamed Fort McIntosh after Colonel James McIntosh who died during the Mexican-

American War. Even though it was called a fort there were no walls, only tents and a few breastworks. A breastwork was a low, temporary fighting position.

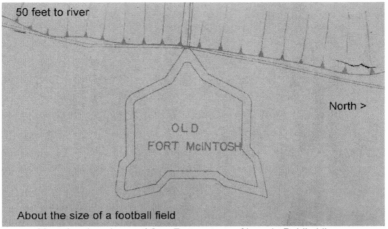

50 feet to river

North >

OLD
FORT McINTOSH

About the size of a football field

Map showing shape of Star Fort curtesy of Laredo Public Library

In 1853 work began on an actual fort. It was shaped like a pentagon with three bastions. One was pointed towards the river overlooking a slight cliff. The ground was considered sufficient to stop any attacks from that direction. Two bastions were built facing east. The fort was still called a "Star Fort" which referred to any fort with bastions.

Wood was scarce so the fort was constructed from dirt piled up to form the walls. The two cannon were placed on platforms on the two east bastions. The fort was more for show since no one ever tried to attack it.

The only hard structure was a stone magazine built underground so enemy fire wouldn't detonate it. The walls were made from sand stone. There were no above ground buildings. The troupes use tents or lived outside. The few horses assigned to Fort McIntosh were kept in corrals built by pilling up brush to create a barrier. During wind storms the dirt piled up forming the walls would be blown away causing a sand storm for anyone caught in it.

Patrols would be sent out to look for bandits or Indians who were hostile to the local inhabitants. Any time tracks were spotted heading inland from the river the troupes would follow trying to determine if this was a raiding party or just horses being moved from one place to another. The troupes were usually mounted infantry and not cavalry. The horses were there to transport the men but not used to fight from. Cavalry, on the other hand were trained to fight from the saddle which was a tremendous advantage but also a huge expense. Cavalry Soldiers received more pay and training than Mounted Infantry, plus the horses were better trained and cared for. A cavalry horse had to be trained to remain calm while fight went on right on top of it. Mounted infantry horses only had to follow their leader down a trail.

Lieutenant Walter Hudson was leading a patrol along the river north from Fort McIntosh. As the detail moved through the brush, they came upon tracks leading away from the river.

The troupes followed to see who was riding through their area of responsibility. They ran into a band of Indians who had come across the river intent on attacking a small settlement. During the gun battle the Lieutenant was severely injured. The Indians broke contact and ran back to the border.

His men managed to get the wounded officer back to the fort. There were no ambulances back then. Not even a wagon. The wounded officer either had to somehow stay in the saddle or he was draped over the horse for transport back to their base.

Lt. Walter Hudson hung onto life for several days before succumbing to his injuries in April, 1850. He was the first soldier to die from wounds suffered in battle while serving at Fort McIntosh.

Forty Texas Rangers arrived at Fort McIntosh enroute to the area northwest of Laredo. They were looking for hostile Indians and they had one man in mind. After restocking their supplies, the Rangers headed out to track down Carne Muerto, Spanish for Dead Meat, a member of the Comanche tribe.

After a few weeks of searching they captured their quarry and transported him back to Fort McIntosh where the Indian was turned over to Captain Sidney Burbank. The captain had Carne Muerto held in the guard house until he could be transferred to San Antonio.

Carne Muerto's wife and mother came to the fort to try arranging his release but the captain refused to allow it. By January Carne Muerto was enroute to San Antonio being escorted by twenty Texas Rangers. Once he was in San Antonio, Carne Muerto was given a trial and then released. He was allowed to return to his family.

Shortly thereafter a delegation of Comanche were brought to the fort to hold Peace Talks but nothing ever came from the meetings.

As more troupes arrived at the fort, it was decided to build some barracks and command offices. There were nearly five-hundred men by 1854. Fort McIntosh was looking more like a military establishment than a camp. The wood needed for construction had to be shipped in from the east. This added an extra expense to the growth of the fort. These buildings were all inside the dirt walls and now gave the fort a more military appearance.

In 1855 Florida was embroiled in The Third Seminole War. Army Scouts and settlers were encroaching on land belonging to the Seminole Indians. The Indians had enough and began attacking forts and settlements. The United States Government began sending troupes into Florida to deal with the situation. Some of these troupes were the men stationed at Fort McIntosh. By 1857 only twenty-six men remained at the fort near Laredo.

With so few men at the fort the government began selling the buildings to the local citizens since wood was a valuable resource. Citizens would bid on a structure and then pay the Quartermaster. Once the building belonged to civilians it had to be taken down and removed from the fort. The wood was transported to where ever it was to be used and rebuilt. By 1858 Fort McIntosh was back to being a bunch of tents inside the dirt walls.

The next year the government all but abandoned the fort leaving it empty for some time.

Bandit activity and Indian raids began to increase. Some of the Indians now living across from Eagle Pass, Texas were Seminoles from the Florida Wars. The locals believed Chief Wild Cat had somewhere around eight-hundred men under his command. In actuality there were around three-hundred Indians living in the area many of whom were from the Kickapoo Tribe.

Pressure from the locals led to an increase in the number of troupes stationed along the border. In 1860 men began to arrive at Fort McIntosh once again. Tents were erected all around the fort until buildings could once more be constructed.

As Fort McIntosh was once more beginning to look like a military establishment the Civil War broke out.

2 THE CHAPEL

Ismael Cuellar started the Laredo paranormal Research Society back in 2002. They were only going to do one investigation, which turned into years of ghost hunts and even looking into UFOs.

Each October the LPRS would do community activities including showing free movies around town at the parks, and teaching citizens about the different things involved in looking into unexplained activity. In 2018, Ismael thought it would be interesting to try a guest event at Fort McIntosh. He contacted the folks at Laredo College and inquired into whether this would be acceptable.

After several weeks of questions and answers the administration agreed to allow the LPRS to hold guest investigations which would be open to the staff and students at the college. The schedule was placed on the college webpage asking those interested to sign up for either a Friday, or Saturday night. There were to be eight nights to choose from.

On October 5, 2018 investigators and guests all met at the Fort Chapel, which was named in honor of Private David B. Barkley Cantu. Private Barkley, also known as David B. Barkley Cantu was born on March 31, 1899. He died in combat on November 9, 1918. Private Barkley was posthumously awarded the Medal of Honor for his heroic actions during World War I in

France. After successfully completing a scouting mission behind enemy lines he drowned while swimming back across the Meuse River. You'll find more about him in a later chapter.

The first night of the Laredo College investigation started off rather slow. The LPRS had already sent out the first group at the chapel. Al was leading the second group of about five people more or less. He was accompanied by Joe Rogerio another Paranormal Investigator who was tagging along.

The first tour was moving just ahead so Al held his people back to allow the first group a good investigation. Too many people moving around in the dark makes for confusion. Nothing really eventful happened in the hallways nor in the kitchen so they continued working their way to the end of the hall.

To the left was a room used as office space which was already being examined by the first group so Al took his team into the room to the right which was empty. The idea was to teach the folks participating in the tour how to conduct a ghost investigation. Al and Joe instructed their group on how to perform an EVP sessions.

The group were told to take lots of photos so they might just catch something paranormal. Any time you're taking "ghost" photos it's a good idea to take more than one of the same object. If you catch some anomaly in one photo it could be just light reflecting off the object. If the anomaly isn't in the second photo this rules out reflections.

Al took his tour up to the second floor for further investigation. The second floor may have been quarters for a general at one time and might have some kind of activity. There were a few EMF spikes but nothing to get excited about.

Each tour was to take about one hour. There were already

people lining up on the sidewalk waiting for their turn so Al led his people back down stairs. He noticed the office was now empty so he asked if the group wanted to give it a try. One of the lady's that was in the group told Al she did not feel comfortable in the office she said "she felt as if something were there." The rest of the team where moving into the office when one young man let out with a sound of pain.

Al moved over to see what was going on. He asked what had happened and the young man stated he'd felt something on his back. The man then said he felt as if he'd been scratched by something. Al asked the young man's girlfriend to lift his shirt. There were scratched across the young man's lower back.

Due to the cramped quarters Joe had stayed just outside the doorway. The man with the scratched was escorted back to the main room to see if he might need first-aid.

Al continued the investigation to see if whatever had attacked the young man was still there but he got no response.

In the main room Ismael, Manny, and Joe had a look, to see what was needed for the man with the scratches. He had six vertical scratches down his lower back.

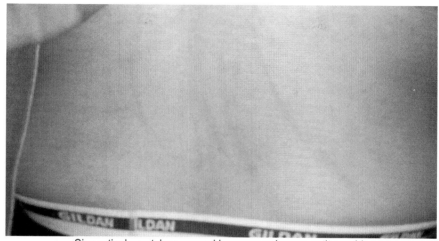
Six vertical scratches caused by some unknown entity or thing.
Photo from LPRS records

Several investigators went down to the office and looked for anything the man might have bumped into or rubbed up against that could have produced these marks but there was nothing there that could account for what had happened.

The young man said he felt fine and didn't need any further attention. He left shortly thereafter with a story to tell about his ghostly encounter.

As Ismael and Al were finishing up for the night it was a common held idea this was going to be the last tour. The student getting scratched would put the whole investigation in a bad light. Instead, this only sparked more interest. More students and staff members began asking to attend, showing more curiosity now that there had been some "real evidence" found of spirit activity. No one wanted to be scratched, but they all wanted to have some form of experience.

I talked to the student that had received the scratches on his back a few weeks later but there was nothing he could add to the story.

During an investigation there are hundreds of photographs taken. With digital cameras you can take as many photos as your memory card can hold. One image shows the front door at the bottom of the stairs.

The front of the Chapel showing the front door at the bottom of the stairs.
Photo curtesy of Laredo Paranormal Research Society.
Image taken by one of the Volunteer Investigators.

There was no one standing by the door when the photo was taken.
Photo curtesy of Laredo Paranormal Research Society.
Image taken by Volunteer Investigator.

If you look closely at the photo you can see a woman standing to the side of the door. Look close and you can see the door through her body.

Back in the 1990s my neighbor Eddy was at Laredo Junior College playing basketball. The game was over and everyone was packing up to leave. He was talking to the coach about things other than bouncing a ball.

An older couple walked across the court. They were dressed in cloths that looked a bit old fashioned but folks do dress the way they wish. The coach looked at the pair and asked if he could help them since the building was not open to the public at the time. The couple never acknowledged his question.

Eddy and the coach both looked at the couple wondering if

there might be some kind of problem. The couple approached the wall without slowing down. Then, as Eddy and the coach watched, the couple walked right through the wall and vanished. What could you say other than that's weird. Eddy and the coach quickly left the ball court.

3 THE GUARDHOUSE

The army brings people together from all over the United States with the purpose of training them to destroy the enemy. This is not a place for singing and dancing. All those rifles and cannon aren't there just for decoration. You train to fight. It can be a violent atmosphere.

When you have large groups of men all stuck in one location for long periods of time it can bring out the worst in some of them. Long periods of inactivity are common and this can lead to discipline problems. Week-ends didn't always mean you had leave. One or two days each month to head to town was considered sufficient. On those occasions the men would try to make up for lost time drinking or running around.

In any city in the United States if a person violates the law they wind up in jail. On a military post they wind up in the Guardhouse. This would be a combination office space and lockup.

According to a map I ran across, Fort McIntosh had several guardhouses. The only guardhouse building still standing is the one built in 1886. The structure consists of four large rooms and three small detention cells.

All the doors and windows were cover by bars making it look very much intimidating. The three small cells had windows placed way up on the wall so prisoners could see it was day time or night time but they couldn't look out and see the fort or anyone walking around outside. The doors to these small cells were solid wood.

On a hot day there was no way to get a breeze coming into

one of these cells and in the few days of winter they would have been icy cold. The only way of relieving themselves would have been a bucket provided to the prisoners that would be emptied once a day.

October 20, 2018. As the sun was going down, the LPRS set up their ghost hunting equipment. The students and staff who had signed up for the tours would arrive and be issued cameras and recorders so they could participate in a ghost investigation.

1886 Guard House during night investigation. Taken using a Sony I.R. camera.

Each group was sent through the building along with one or two LPRS members to keep an eye on things so no one got hurt, and to answer questions. The people on the tours would be doing most of the investigation. We were just there to help out and give advice when needed.

24

A young girl, Sofi, who showed up each night to participate in every ghost tour she could, was the first one through the massive door to the first large room. About ten students ranging in age from eighteen to twenty-five filed in behind her.

The rooms were all connected by passageways with bared doors but these were all locked. You could look from room to room but not walk through. To move from one room to the next it was necessary to go outside and walk across the porch.

At one time the guardhouse had been used as a children's museum. Then the building was used for storage. There were a collection of antique bottles all sitting on the floor. In the center room, someone knocked over one of the bottles which made a loud bang. This was followed by a scream and a sudden exodus from the guardhouse. All of the students had ran as if being chased by a ghost.

I looked in to see if anyone was still in there. There was Sofi holding out an E.M.F. detector trying to see if she could capture evidence of ghosts. The students had run away leaving her behind. She was so intent on doing what she was there for she didn't notice she was alone.

The students all looked back and forth realizing they had been spooked by nothing and made their way back inside. I wonder what they thought when they saw Sofi was the only one who didn't get scared and run?

Ismael was in the main room of the guardhouse showing guests how to use the thermal camera. One of the women in the group said she could "feel" someone standing next to her. Then, to show her appreciation to the spirit the woman said, "I would like to thank you for your service."

As she was speaking Ismael aimed the thermal camera at her

face. He could see something was moving about her as she was speaking. The image on the thermal camera looked like her skin was being sectioned off into many small squares, like pixilation. This only showed up while she was speaking and only on her face. Once she had finished her image returned to normal.

Later that same night Ismael set up the Mel Meter in the central room.

The Mel-8704 was designed and built by Gary Galka. His eldest daughter Melissa was born in 1987 and died in 2004. This is why it is the 8704. After her death she began making contact with her family so Gary put this meter together to make communications easier. The meter is a dual purpose unit that measures both E.M.F. and Temperature changes simultaneously.

The students all gather around to watch and listen as Ismael asked for any spirits to make their presence known. Being a jail, Ismael asked if any of the spirits had been prisoners here. He asked in both English and Spanish.

Being an American Fort, would there have been Spanish speaking prisoners kept here?

On June 16, 1916 a band of one hundred Mexican soldiers from either the Carrancistas or the Seditionists decided to attack a small military post in San Ygnacio, Texas. What they didn't know was a large detachment of soldiers moving from Fort McIntosh, enroute to Fort Ringgold had stopped to spend the night in San Ygnacio. As the Mexican soldiers crossed the river they were met by a superior force and during the skirmish many men were killed. Three American soldiers and six Mexican soldiers were dead and several from both sides were seriously injured. As daylight came over the small town the United States soldiers had managed to capture several of their attackers. The prisoners were transported back to Fort McIntosh.

Once on the fort grounds, Texas Rangers were called to the fort and from there, the prisoners were transported to the Webb County Jail.

One of the wounded soldiers from Fort McIntosh died the next day from his injuries and the District Attorney used this as a reason to try the Mexican Soldiers in Webb County, even though the raid had taken place in Zapata Country.

The invaders were found guilty of murder. As they awaited execution an appeals court stepped in and declared the prisoners could not be tried in a state court because Texas was in fact at war with Mexico and therefore the prisoners had to face a military court. The entire company that had faced the invaders had been reassigned to Fort Bliss in El Paso and so none of the witnesses were called to testify during the appeals trial.

The Texas Rangers turned the prisoners over to Colonel Ferguson at Fort McIntosh. After a few weeks of debate, the military said the United States was not at war with Mexico and this meant Texas was not at war either. The prisoners were then released at Nuevo Laredo where they received a hero's welcome.

The reports on the raid vary from a few dozen bandits or soldiers up to one hundred. Some said they were Constitutionalists but General Alfredo Ricaut, of the Constitutional Army, was adamant about not allowing bandit activity in the United States. This story is the most often stated so we'll go with it as being as close to what happened as we can find.

So Ismael asking the spirits in Spanish was appropriate. The meter would give off a high pitched sound after each question. The questions were all yes or no answers and the spirit was asked to make one sound for yes and two for no.

As Ismael was asking a question suddenly the meter jumped from the large wooden box it had been resting on. It fell to the floor at his feet. No one had been close enough to knock the device over let alone get it over the side and onto the floor. One of the students in the tour was filming the whole time but we never found the moment the EMF fall. The camera had been focused on Ismael and not the meter.

Ismael theorized, having so many untrained investigators in one location with so many emotions, the spirits were feeding off their energy and this was leading to a lot of activity.

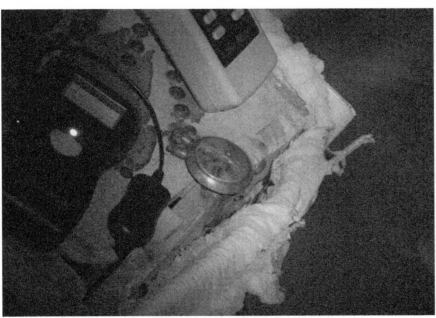

Even though it looks like a watch this was a fancy lighter that was loaned to the LPRS by the family of General Haynes.
Photo compliments of the LPRS

The family of General Haynes loaned the LPRS a cigarette lighter from the 1900s. It was very fancy and valuable. Troupes smoked. At one time smoking was considered to be good for you. When I was at Fort Knox a carton of cigarettes cost $4.50. At one time you would receive cigarettes in "C" Ration packages. Just about everyone in the military smoked.

The fancy cigarette lighter was placed on the wooden box along with a few cigarettes. We also stepped outside and once in a while took a sniff of the air to see if we caught the smell of burning tobacco.

The ghosts didn't use any of the cigarettes so they were left behind at the end of the tour.

Left to right. Noehmi and Sofia Juarez, age 11.
Photo from the Laredo Paranormal Research Society

Sofi is one of the future ghost investigators. Her mother, Noehmi, works at Laredo College. They showed up for every LPRS ghost tour that was held at the old fort. Not only was Sofi there ready to go looking for the unknown, she brought some of her own investigating tools.

For her birthday she asked for and received a digital thermometer that is used to find anomalous temperature spikes, and a voice recorder used for EVP sessions.

When she turned nine Sofi began to wonder if ghosts and spirits were real and was there any way of proving it. She got started by reading books on ghosts, like "The Laredo Paranormal Research Society" and watching T.V. shows like "Ghost Adventures" For just plain entertainment she watches "Stranger Things" not to be mistaken for the podcast "Strange Things with Chris James." "Full House" and "Fuller House" are some of her favorites.

When asked if the idea of disembodied spirits lurking around her was scary, Sofi said, "No, because I have always felt things like disembodied spirits in my home since I was 7 years old and I have gotten used to it."

A year ago while her cousin was over visiting the two girls saw a shadowy figure in her closet. It was a bit frightening at first but then it was just a shadow.

With Christmas just around the corner Sofi is hoping for an Ovilus, which is an electronic speech-synthesis device which creates words depending on electromagnetic waves in the air around us. She also hopes to get a Mel-8704 meter. The Mel Meter was developed just for paranormal research. It reads both EMF and temperature. She's going to need a bigger backpack for all her gear.

One of her best friends is afraid of ghosts and the other was disappointed she missed out on the ghost tours at the college.

During the Guardhouse investigation, Sofi was the first one through the door. She was there to look for ghosts. A group of students from Laredo College followed behind her. In the next room over someone knocked a bottle over making a loud noise.

This caused one of the students to scream. One thing led to another and suddenly all the students were running for the door. The guardhouse was cleared out of everyone except Sofi. She was still in there looking for the former residents.

I asked her how this made her feel? She said "I didn't really care, but in my mind I was just thinking 'wimps".

Since she was on every ghost tour at the college Sofi was able to see a few light orbs. She also got to take part in a conversation involving Lieutenant Karl, a former soldier who I'm now trying to track down in the old fort records. The entire conversation was done using the "Spirit Box." She is there to get answers and this is what she's going to do.

I asked Sofi if someone were to ask her about a possible haunting, what she would tell them as far as advice?

She said, "Well if they asked me about a haunting in their house but they did not want help, I would say to try to investigate yourself and tell them some of the equipment to use to help them investigate."

She went on to say, "But if they did want help, I would say contact LPRS and if they did not want it in their house I would say contact a priest. If the person needed to get help because of a possession I would say contact an exorcist."

When asked about UFOs, Sofi said she believed in them but had never seen one herself. She wasn't interested in Bigfoot but she did say there might be a giant hair covered creature out there but she wasn't interested in going to have a look.

When not looking into the paranormal, Sofi like to read, listen to music, sing, write poetry, and do martial arts training.

4 THE WAR BETWEEN THE STATES

In 1836 Sam Houston became the first president of Texas after defeating Santa Ana at the Battle of San Jacinto. In 1846 he became a United Sates Senator once Texas became a state. In 1859 Sam Huston was elected Governor of Texas. When Abraham Lincoln won the November 1860 presidential election, Southern states began voting to seceded from the United States. These southern states formed the Confederate States of America.

In 1861 Texas citizens began campaigning to be removed from the Union as well. Their stated reason was the United States didn't do enough to protect the citizens living along the southern border. The people living in Laredo unanimously voted for secession.

On February 1, 1861 the Texas convention voted to secede from the United States, and Houston proclaimed that Texas was once again an independent republic. Houston wasn't opposed to leaving the Union but he didn't like the idea of joining the Confederacy. When the Texas Legislature voted to join the Confederacy, Houston refused to recognize the convention's authority. Houston refused to swear an oath of loyalty to the Confederacy, leading to the legislature declaration that the governorship was therefore vacant.

Sam Houston refused to leave office but he also refused to

take any action to stay. The Union offered to send troupe to be placed at his disposal which he also refused.

With Houston out of the way, Texas joined the Confederate States of America on March 2, 1861.

Union troupes stationed at Fort McIntosh were told to make preparations to abandon the fort. Anything not moveable was to be turned over to Charles Callahan.

Once the fort was no longer in Union hands Captain Santos Benavides was told to take possession. The 3rd and 33rd Confederate Cavalry were under his command.

The battles between Union and Confederate troupes were far away. The troupes stationed at Fort McIntosh patrolled the border looking for bandits and hostile Indians.

The government in Mexico was torn between supporting the Confederacy or supporting the Union.

Juan Nepomuceno Cortina Goseacochea, also known as Chino Cortina, was the Governor of Tamaulipas, Mexico and a General in the Mexican Army. His family had received land grants on both sides of the Rio Grande so when the border was established as being the river he was angered by those he felt had stolen his family land.

During the Civil War he used his position to authorize bandit raids into Texas. In May 1861 General Cortina invaded Carrizo Texas, now named Zapata Texas.

When word of the invasion reached Fort McIntosh Captain Benavides took twenty-seven men and road to Carrizo.

Refugio Benavides, Santos' brother left the fort enroute to meet up with his brother. Knowing the roads to Carrizo were now controlled by Mexican troupes, Refugio crossed into

Mexico, then road south east and joined his brother.

Lt. Callahan left Fort McIntosh with an additional thirty-six men and road to support Captain Benavides. Once the three units had formed up they attacked the troupes holding Texas territory driving them back into Mexico. This was known as the Battle of Carrizo.

General Cortina was mad at being thrown out of Texas. He then began sending bandit raids into The United States. Bandit Chief Antonio Ochoa rode into Zapata County. He and his men hung Judge Ygnacio Vela. Once they had terrorized the citizens the bandits road back into Mexico where they thought they were safe.

Captain Benavides took fifty-five men and crossed into Mexico. The CSA troupes tracked the bandits to Mesquital Lealeño, near Camargo. In the dead of night the Confederate troupes attacked the bandits killing many and taking the rest into custody. The bandit captives were tried and executed for murder.

When word spread that bandits weren't safe even in their home country the raids all but came to an end. For his handling the bandit problem so well Captain Benavides was promoted to Colonel. His brother Refugio was promoted to Captain.

By 1863 Union troupes managed to capture Brownsville, Texas cutting off a major shipping route used by the Confederate States. Goods being shipped out from the south to help support the Confederacy, and Gold and arms being shipped in were now having to find new shipping routes. Laredo and Rio Grande City both filled the gap.

The goods enroute to Matamoros and then Bagdad Mexico, which was the port used by the Confederacy, needed to travel through the northern state of Tamaulipas Mexico. France had invaded Mexico in 1861. This tied up most of the Mexican military trying to drive the French out of their country. General Cortina was still supporting the Union.

Colonel Benavides managed to contact bandits in Mexico and convince them to help protect the Confederate shipments in return for gold and weapons. Shipments of cotton could now make their way to Bagdad and then be placed on ships enroute for New York. Yes the Union was buying goods from Mexico which had originated in the Confederacy. The gold used to purchase cotton was then shipped back to the Confederate State of America. Since most of Mexico supported the Union the Federal Navy never interfered in shipping coming out of Bagdad.

Fort McIntosh was still one of the lest sought after posts in all of Texas. The ground didn't support much vegetation so any food had to be shipped in. In March, 1864 Colonel Benavides sent a large portion of his cavalry north to graze their horses. On the 18, Major Alfred Holt led a Union force of 200 men from Brownsville, Texas, with orders to destroy the 5,000 bales of cotton stacked at the San Agustín Plaza. The cotton was enroute to New York City by way of Bagdad, Mexico.

With only forty-two infantry troupes, Colonel Benavides set out to stop the Union troupes. He gave orders for Captain Benavides to burn the cotton should the Colonel fail. I know this sounds contradictory, to burn the cotton so the Union troupes couldn't burn it. I very seriously doubt the colonel knew what the union troupes were coming to Laredo for. He probably thought they were coming to seize the cotton for their own purposes.

The colonel lead his men out of town and took up position on the top of a hill. The union troupes attacked and were driven off. With just a handful of men the colonel kept the union out of

Laredo. The Union troupes tried twice more and each time were repelled.

By nightfall the confederate soldiers who had been away grazing their horses returned to Fort McIntosh. As they were riding into town Captain Benavides told the townsfolk to ring the church bells.

Major Alfred Holt, hearing the bells in town, came to the conclusion reinforcements had arrived. Having been driven off three times by the smaller force, he knew his men would not fare any better running up against several hundred confederate soldiers.

Early the next morning, Colonel Benavides sent out scouts to check on the union troupes and see if they had been reinforced. The scouts snuck about looking for any sign of the enemy. When no soldiers could be seen the scouts rode through the brush where the Union Troupes had been camped. They discovered the site where the soldiers had been was now empty.

Colonel Benavides was proclaimed the victor of the Battle of Laredo.

The LPRS had been doing archeological investigations as well as paranormal. The owner of a ranch that was now in town contacted them and said they were welcome to have a look on his property but the land was scheduled for construction soon. They were given one week to sweep the area with their metal detectors.

It was a cold day as the team showed up and began their hunt for underground artifacts. If you've never handled a metal detector you find a lot of old discarded things that are worth less than the amount of trouble to dig them up. Beer cans and nails.

Old car parts and in Texas, lots of discarded oil field equipment.

As Ismael and Rick were working their way across the field, they came into a sphere of warm air. It hung there in the middle of nowhere like a cloud of hot gas. Rick was able to find the edge with his hands. The heated mass was roughly the shape of a ball and about five feet across. Seeing as it was January and only fifty degrees out the warm air mass felt kind of good, but spooky. The hot air mass began to move one way and then the other, then it was gone. Just maybe this was the spirit of a horse killed during the Battle of Laredo. The gang had found parts to a bridle and some harness hardware.

All in all they found a lot of old items that looked as if a battle had been fought there.

Some artifacts found during archaeological investigation.

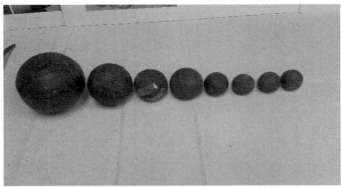

Cannon balls found at the dig site

Fort McIntosh became a Laredo Junior College in 1947. The campus consisted of a few old building from when it was a military fort and some new construction to accommodate students. Student housing was in a one story building on the north side of the campus.

Late one night a female student was asleep in her dorm when she awoke with a start. There, at the foot of her bed stood a man in Civil War uniform. He stood there for a few seconds and then faded away. She tried to convince herself it was just a dream but the image stuck with her from then on.

The President of Laredo College has a house next door to the Chapple. The LPRS was invited to do an investigation and tour of the building.

The equipment was set out on a table in the basement where the guests would gather to begin their night. Ismael was giving instructions the guests on how to use the electronic equipment. As he was standing near the stairs coming into the basement from outside, the doors suddenly slammed shut right behind him.

There was no wind at the time and no one could have pushed the doors shut without being seen by all the guests. This helped get everyone in the mood to go looking for spirits.

During the investigations, the LPRS team had mounted a camera on a remote controlled toy car. There was a tunnel on the east end of the basement that needed looking into. The history of who built the tunnel and when is lost to time but today it had pipes running through it. The tunnel runs at a south-easterly direction.

The toy was driven into the tunnel looking for anything odd. As it was moving along, a mist formed right in front of the camera. The mist hung there for a few seconds and then faded away.

5 RECONSTRUCTION YEARS

With the end of the Civil War the Union troupes moved back into Fort McIntosh. Captain Duke took over as Provost of Laredo. He tried to clean up the city in an effort to make life better for the folks living outside the fort.

At the time sanitation was limited. Water was distributed by a wagon that carried water from the river to the citizens. The people living in Laredo had little regard for things like garbage pickup or disposal of waste. If a home owner were to slaughter a cow, the entrails and discards would remain in the streets until dogs and other scavengers carried it away. At times the aroma was quite intense. The army tried to enforce sanitation laws until such time as the city officials took over.

Captain Duke discovered all of the elected officials in Webb County were ineligible to hold office due to either not being citizens or having participated in criminal activity.

Captain Benavidez continued leading patrols along the border looking for bandits and hostile Indians. The people living in the area were kept relatively safe compared to other border regions. These patrols continued until the unit was disbanded in 1874. By then the U.S. Army had taken over these duties.

The US army was segregated. There were all black companies and all white companies. The "Buffalo Soldiers" of the 10th Cavalry, were black soldiers. No one knows if the name was due to the men having curly black hair like the mane of a buffalo or because the soldiers fought so valiantly and fiercely that the Indians revered them as they did the mighty buffalo.

The American Buffalo is actually called a Bison. Those huge, shaggy animals seen in the west are Bison-Bison. They are in the same family group as the Asian Water Buffalo, Bubalus-Bubalis, and the African Cape Buffalo, Syncerus-Caffer. Bison are not closely related to those species, making the common name buffalo misleading, and Bison Soldiers doesn't have the same ring to it.

In 1870, the 10th Cavalry were sent to Fort McIntosh. Many of the locals in Laredo were a bit put off by these different looking men but soon grew accustomed to them. As always there were some who thought black soldiers should not be in town.

As with any military city, places popped up around town that catered to the wishes of the men at the fort. Strong drinks, gambling and, as Terry Pratchett would say, "women of negotiable affections."

The police tended to turn a blind eye to these activities. The thought being the soldiers needed a place to enjoy themselves. As long as the partying didn't get out of hand, and there were sometimes a few dollars to be made on the side, These "entertainment houses" were allowed to unofficially operate.

General William Tecumseh Sherman arrived at Fort McIntosh in 1882. He had arrived in Laredo to participate in the Grand Opening of a temporary railroad bridge connecting Laredo and Nuevo Laredo by crossing the Rio Grande River.

In Laredo there were two political parties. The Botas or

Boots, and the Guaraches, or Sandals. The Botas were made up of some of the upper society of Laredo as well as new arrivals who had moved to the town after the war. The Guaraches were made of the other half of the upper society but played themselves off as being the "working man's party." Both parties did their best to villainize the other.

As the 1886 elections drew near both parties began to accuse the other of illegal activities including importing citizens from Mexico to vote in the elections. At each and every rally alcohol flowed freely leading to many altercations. These altercations became violent enough to instill a feeling of dread amongst the party members. The members began going around town armed.

The Guaraches had been the dominant party for many years but in 1886 things changed. The Botas took nearly every position after the votes were counted. As the victory celebration was in full swing a mock funeral was to be held showing the demise of the Guaraches. Cooler heads prevailed and managed to stay the outlandish parade.

On April 6, 1886 the Botas changed their minds and began a funeral procession along the streets of Laredo. The Guaraches seeing what was happening began followed behind yelling out insults. Several members of the Guaraches were dragging a yellow cannon along with them. Alcohol and firearms were abundant in both parties.

As the Botas assembled in San Agustin Plaza to finalize the mock funeral the Guaraches rolled the cannon to the other end of the plaza. With so many drunken zealots on both sides it was only a matter of time before someone fired a shot.

The cannon was fired and reloaded. Rifles and pistols were fired from the streets as well as the roof tops. A riot had broken out threating to destroy the town.

At Fort McIntosh, Colonel Bernard could hear the gun fire. It sounded as if a major battle was taking place. He sent scouts into town to judge the condition of the situation and readied his men. At this time most of the 10th Cavalry was made up of what were known as Buffalo Soldiers, black enlisted men who stayed in the army after the Civil War.

When word got back to the colonel that many if not most of the shooting was being done by, what to them, were Mexican citizens, the rule of Posse Comitatus Act was thrown out.

The Posse Comitatus, or power of the county, is the group of people, posse, mobilized by the conservator of peace, usually the sheriff, to suppress lawlessness or defend the county. In the United States, a federal statute known as the Posse Comitatus Act, enacted in 1878, forbade the use of the United States Army as a Posse Comitatus or for law enforcement purposes without the approval of Congress.

Colonel Bernard, thinking the gun fire was an attack being coordinated by Mexico, marched on the town intent on repelling an international invasion.

The army arrived causing most of the rioters to flee. The soldiers began moving from street to street disarming anyone they encountered. The citizens who had stayed out of the skirmish cheered as the soldiers did their duty to stop any further destruction of property, or loss of life.

Many of the rioters were seen running for the border. Whether these were in fact Mexican citizens or U.S. citizens wishing to avoid arrest is unknown. This did bolster Colonel Bernard's assertion that the riot had been an international incursion.

All that night the infantry continued to tour the streets as the cavalry patrolled the river banks to stop any further attacks.

By morning the number of people wounded or killed was tabulated. Someone, somewhere, wrote it down and then things got messed up. One report said only six men were killed and thirty wounded. Another report said thirty men were killed and over a hundred wounded. There is one report of over one hundred dead. Firing a cannon into a crowded street would have wounded many men and killed several as well.

Until someone comes up with the original records on casualties from the riot we will not know the actual number of casualties. The soldiers from Fort McIntosh are credited with stopping a far worse outcome.

Small Pox is a disease that has killed thousands of people over the last few millennia. Once an outbreak was discovered there was a 35 present chance of death from the pox. If you were lucky enough to survive there was a great chance of scaring from the pustules.

In the 1500s China had come up with preventive measure that was one hundred present viable. Powdered small pox scabs were blown up the nostrils of the recipient who would then develop a mild case of the pox and be immune from then on.

In 1796, Edward Jenner realized the women who milked cows for a living would develop a form of cow pox which would then give the women immunity from the small pox virus.

Nuevo Laredo discovered a small pox outbreak in 1898. The mayor of Laredo, Louis Christen, asked the government of Nuevo Laredo to take steps to quarantine the neighborhoods where the outbreak was found. Unfortunately it was too late and the virus spread across the river. The first case in Laredo was the daughter of a railroad conductor named Kerl. Kerl was a prominent German name found in Northern Mexico.

By January 1899 there were over one hundred cases of small pox in Laredo. Most of these cases were found on the south east side of town near Zacate Creek. Dr. Blunt, the State Health Official, came to Laredo to see about getting the situation under control. He found few people in the area where most cases were found had been inoculated.

Once a person was diagnosed as having small pox they would be transported to a hospital unit called a Pest House. Since there was no cure, the patients would be housed there until they either recovered or died. Many relatives of the patients didn't know the disease was passed from person to person by either inhalation of airborne virus particles, such as microscopic droplets from the oral, nasal, or pharyngeal mucosa of an infected person, or by contact with infected bodily fluids in clothing or bed coverings.

Everything the patients were in contact with had to be burned but some families refused.

The Texas Rangers were there to help enforce the removal and quarantine of anyone found with the disease. As Dr. Blunt and his associates arrived at one neighborhood they were met by residents who refused to allow them in. A struggle ensued leading to Ranger Captain Rogers being shot in the shoulder. He fired one shot killing his assailant.

An order arrived at the local hardware store for one thousand round of buckshot to be delivered to the Zacate Creek neighborhood were the altercation had taken place. Instead of fulfilling the order the manager contacted the sheriff.

Sheriff Ortiz obtained a search warrant to enter the homes in the neighborhood. There were over one hundred neighbors all there armed and ready to keep the search warrant from being executed. The sheriff contacted Fort McIntosh requesting their assistance. The 10th cavalry under Captain Ayers arrived bringing with them a Gatling gun as a show of force. Seeing the soldiers arriving en masse the people of the neighborhood made a run for the border.

The soldiers assisted in a house to house search for anyone showing signs of infection. This did fall outside the Posse Comitatus Act but their assistance helped stop an otherwise deadly outbreak from becoming even worse.

The men who had swum the river into Mexico were met by units from the Mexican Army who rounded them up and returned them to the Texas Rangers waiting at the bridge. Once the infected had been removed the citizens were allowed to return to their homes.

No one wanted their property being turned into a pest house. Once the infection was in the structure, the building would be useless for any other purpose. Needing someplace to house the sick, Laredo Health Department arranged to borrow tents from Fort McIntosh. These tents were set up near Zacate Creek and east of town.

Patients and medical staff were living in tents until the disease ran its course. Once patients were no longer infectious they would be released to go back home. The doctors and nurses from out of town continued living in the tents until the small pox outbreak was over.

The tents were not new and some were in bad shape. During a rain storm many of the tents leaked so bad the patients and staff used umbrellas to stay dry as they sat inside the canvas structures.

By April 1899 the quarantine was lifted in Laredo. The tents used for pest houses were shipped to Nuevo Laredo to be steam cleaned before being sent back to the soldiers at the fort.

By 1899 Captain Ayers had become the commanding officer in charge of Fort McIntosh. He had made a name for himself while serving in Cuba. When Teddy Roosevelt charged up San Juan Hill in 1898, Captain Ayers and the 10th Cavalry had been right there with him.

Thomas Reeds had a problem with black soldiers. He'd been at Fort McIntosh for years and thought only white men should be allowed in the army. One night Reeds got drunk and began causing problems.

Captain Ayers sent Lieutenant Brown to arrest the disorderly soldier. When Reeds discovered he was being arrested by a black man he pulled a gun and began firing. The Lieutenant dove for cover and was hit in the back.

The captain sent a detail of men from the 10th Cavalry armed with carbines to deal with the drunken soldier. When the smoke cleared Reeds was bleeding severely from both legs. He was taken to the fort hospital where he was treated by the same doctor that had just worked on Lieutenant Brown. Due to Reeds' injuries, both legs were amputated.

Lieutenant Brown recovered and returned to his duties. Reeds wound up in a wheelchair and military prison.

The people living in Laredo considered this to be just a conflict amongst the troupes but one newspaper began calling for the removal of the soldiers of the 10th Cavalry. "The Chaparral" began making wild claims about how black men would run rampant through town if not removed from the fort.

As far as the average person in town, soldiers were soldiers, no matter their color. Everyone appreciated the money they spent while on leave in town.

The Chaparral continued trying to stir things up for years before closing their doors. The paper was gone long before the soldiers of the 10th Cavalry.

Life got back to normal and the troupes at Fort McIntosh began to get bored. There is nothing worse for moral than to have nothing to do. It can lead to unsoldierly conduct.

Six months after helping out with the small pox outbreak a group of soldiers from the 10th Cavalry were in town on leave. They had gathered at a house of ill repute. "Women of Negotiable Affections" as Terry Pratchett called them. A brothel. Drinking and horseplay led to a police officer being called to the house. Drunken soldiers can be a mess to deal with since not only are they in good physical shape but they have been trained to fight. The police got the upper hand and sent the soldiers back to the fort.

This should have been the end of the matter but the soldiers felt slighted. After arming themselves they returned to Laredo looking for a fight.

The soldiers managed to find one police officer and beat him up. They then ran around town making a big scene before stumbling back to their barracks.

The commanding officer. Hearing from the Laredo Police about a band of drunken armed soldiers running about town called for an immediate head count.

All the soldiers were formed up and the NCOs checked for missing men. Everyone was present or accounted for. The commanding officer wanted to know who had entered town armed and assaulted a police man. No one would confess. A check of the armory found the lock was broken but all of the weapons were in place.

Unable to find out who was to blame the commander sent word to Washington stating the situation in Laredo was unruly and it would be best to simply close the fort and reassign everyone to San Antonio.

When word reached the citizens in Laredo the fort was being considered for closure they send word to Washington requesting the fort stay open because it was a vital means of security along the border. This and they relished the income brought to town by the soldiers and the contracts with the military.

Washington decided Fort McIntosh should continue operating for the time being. They even began to improve the fort making life at the facility a bit more bearable for the men stationed there.

By 1900, the 10th Cavalry had been transferred to the Philippians. Soldiers making trouble in town continued if not increased. It got to a point the M.P.s would patrol town along with the Laredo Police.

In 1908 a company drilled down to an artesian well bringing fresh water to the fort. Up until this time water was drawn from the river. The Rio Grande passes many farms and ranches as it flows towards the Gulf of Mexico. As it goes, it picks up dirt and debris, along with things dropped by cattle and other animals. The water turns brown as it approached Laredo.

With the new well troupes could get water from a clean source. Once the well was in, Laredo asked for the same company to put in more wells for the city.

An electric line was run from Laredo Electric and Railway into Fort McIntosh. For the first time electric lights were turned on at the post exchange. The rest of the fort had to wait a little longer to get power.

First Sergeant Jacobs had a small house on the south east side of the fort. In September 1908 he invited Master Sergeant Sharb to come by and enjoy the evening listening to a gramophone and drinking a few beers. They were both from Company H, of the 19th Infantry. The two sergeants were considered to be close friends having served together for years.

Around 10:45, Sharb excused himself in order to return to his own place. Shortly thereafter Sharb returned to Jacobs' house and, standing out front, yelled for the First Sergeant to come outside. When Jacobs stepped out the door he was confronted by his friend waving a pistol and yelling.

Sharb said "This one is for you." He leveled the revolver and fired hitting Jacobs in the face. The bullet entered his mouth and exited through his check.

Sharb then said "And this one is for me." Placed the gun against his head and pulled the trigger. The bullet entered his brain and he fell to the ground.

Jacobs was able to get to his feet. He staggered to the hospital under his own power. Once there he was treated for a gunshot wound to the check and a broken jaw.

Master Sergeant Sharb was brought to the hospital and treated for the head wound but he died later that night.

An inquest was held to try to find out why the Master

Sergeant shot his friend and then himself but nothing was ever determined to be the cause of the assault. After recovering from his wounds, First Sergeant Jacobs said he didn't know why his friend had decided to try to kill him or why the Master Sergeant took his own life.

6 ARECHIGA HALL

Arechiga Hall is the oldest building still standing at Laredo College. Built in 1880 it was one of three buildings used to house troupes. Each building was a two story brick structure with a basement used for storage and maintenance and a large attic.

Arechiga Hall as it looked in 1917. You can see the line of
Army barracks along the street.
Postcard compliments of the Laredo Public Library.

As the buildings grew old, and newer more modern construction methods came along, the barracks were torn down to allow for newer buildings to be put up. The sole remaining building was named for Domingo Arechiga who had been the President of Laredo Junior College from 1974 to 1985.

The staff working in the old building began telling of strange sightings and sounds as they worked in their offices or moved about the building.

Ismael Cuellar managed to get permission for the Laredo Paranormal Research Society to conduct combination ghost tours and investigations inside the hall.

The gang arrived early to set up all of the equipment. Cameras and recorders were there to be used by the staff and students wishing to learn and participate in a ghost investigation.

After a briefing on how to use the equipment and the proper procedures in conduction an investigation the participants were sent up to begin their ghost hunts in the attic.

Students in the attic during an EVP session.
Photo taken using Sony IR camera.

It was worm outside and very hot in the attic. The students

and staff would rotate every hour. The LPRS Investigators spent nearly four hours in the cramped and stifling space. This combined with climbing the stairs led to an aerobic workout. Everyone was glad to get back downstairs and into the air conditioning.

One suspected reason for the ghostly presence is what happened back in 1986 or 87. Two women working at the hall died in a car crash during their lunch break.

The fire alarm had gone off during work hours. Everyone was ushered outside as the Fire Department arrived to investigate. With everyone standing around outside, it was decided to take an early lunch break. As the two women were returning to the college a car ran a stop light and hit them. They both died instantly. It sounds as if they may have returned to the college after all.

The LPRS uses a new technology in some of their investigations. It's call the Structured Light Sensor or SLS. This device sends out thousands of laser beams which are then interpreted by the computer. Anything breaking the beams will then show up in whatever form it is in. The LPRS have the computer hooked to a large T.V. monitor so everyone in the room can see what the SLS is catching.

During the test, I saw what looked like a figure standing beside me on the screen. I reached over and tried touching the image. It would jerk back as my hands got close. It then bobbed up and down. It looked like it could feel my touch even though I never felt anything next to me.

Dayna sitting in the laser grid from the SLS. These pinpoint lights are only visible to the IR camera and computer. If anything brakes the light pattern it will be interpreted as a stick figure on the screen.

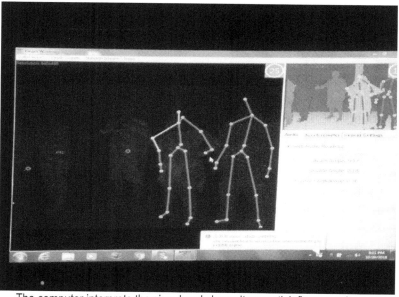

The computer interprets the signal and shows it as a stick figure on the screen. It will only pick up on the two closest images to the sensor. You can see four images at the top right of the screen.

During one of the sessions Dayna decided to try offering a treat to one of the spirits.

Using an EMF detector the team had asked how old one of the spirits was. They started at ten and worked down. The flashing lights said the spirit was eight. Dayna had brought some candy along with her and would offer it to the spirit. The EMF detector would flash once for "yes" and twice for "no." She asked if the spirit wanted her to give candy to one of the students in her group. It flashed "no." She asked if the spirit wanted all the candy and it flashed "yes."

This activity continued until Dayna ran out of treats. When it was time to leave all the candy was left sitting on the desk.

Here is one of the end of tour photos from the LPRS archives.
The painting on the wall is President Domingo Arechiga.

Look at the image standing behind everyone. When the photo was taken there was no one there.

As each tour was ending Ismael would have all the guests stand together for a photo. This was to go into the LPRS archives. Each night there would be four or five tours depending on the number of folks who showed up.

Once everyone was home, the photos are looked over to see how they came out and if there was anything odd to be seen. Standing behind the group from Arechiga Hall there was an unexpected guest. Based on the angle of the photo and the distance the shape looks like a smaller person, maybe a child?, standing by the back door.

Using photo enhancement software the photo was examined several times. It was definitely there but the image couldn't be improved.

On occasion the Laredo Paranormal Research Society bring in guest investigators. They come from other groups in distant towns or they are independent investigators or researchers.

Christopher Juarez was invited to come along by his sister, Dayna. He was at the Arechiga Hall on October 12, 2018. Here is his story in his own words.

"Hello my name is Christopher Juarez I am a guest investigator for the Laredo Paranormal Research Society. I've been with the LPRS for about a year and mostly due photography for them. This is what I experienced at the Laredo College while in the Arechiga Hall."

"It was toward the end of the night, around 12 AM. We had one last tour left before we would wrap everything up at the Arechiga Hall. The Lead Investigator asked if I could take the last tour around the building. I agreed to take them. Another guest investigator, who was also a medium, decided to help me with the group. We went to the attic on the 3rd floor and nothing really out of the ordinary happened."

After a few minutes we moved down to the 2nd floor. On the second floor something strange happen and to this day, I can't explain what happened or how it happened."

"We enter the second floor and I look to my right which leads to a hallway and to my left is another hallway. I decided to head down the hallway to the left first. I lead the group down that hallway and nothing happens except a few words from the Ovilus."

"I decided to move in the other direction, down the other hallway. As I was walking towards the corridor my vision started to get foggy so I tried to clear my eyes by rubbing them. As soon as I did this, the medium said that there were two spirits in front of me. I asked anyone in the group with me if they could see anything using the night vision or thermal camera or if they could see fog in the air?"

"The group replied saying no there was nothing there and they did not see any fog. I decided to head down the end of the hallway with the medium following right behind me. As we get to the end of the hall, the fog I could see cleared up. As I turned around, the fog was back. I turn back around toward the medium and the fog was not there."

"Once more she said 'There are two spirits.' As soon as she said that the fog came back from the top corner of the hall covering the medium. Everywhere around me was foggy and blurry. I couldn't see anything and my eyesight was getting worse to the point that I could not see anything. The medium advised me to get out of there because the spirits were trying to attach themselves to me."

"I decide to leave this hallway and move away from what was going on. I headed out of the hallway and my vision started clearing up. I turned to look back at where I had been, the fog was following me."

"The medium screamed at me to leave because the spirits were following me. Just then I decided to get off of the second floor completely and head down to the first floor."

"I started to make the sign of the cross and pray the 'Saint Michael Prayer' to get rid of anything trying to attach itself to me. The group that I was with finally came down with the medium in tow. She comes up to me and ask if I was ok? She looked closely at me and said, 'You are fine, nothing is with you anymore. But just in case, say a prayer and go outside and open yourself up to the wind element to cleanse yourself of any and all bad energy."

"That was my experience at Laredo College and the Arechiga Hall…."

Martha Oviedo-Venegas

Martha Oviedo-Venegas was a student at Laredo Community College back in the 1990s. To make ends meet she took a job at the Arechiga hall working on the second floor. This was where the Social and Behavioral Department had their offices.

The desk was right across the hallway from the stairs leading up to the attic. The attic had a large room with a table and a few chairs but it was seldom used since it was hot just about year round. Hot as in up around one hundred degrees. There was no air conditioning up there.

The staff would all hear what sounded like people moving around upstairs. There would be bumps and creeks. Footsteps going from place to place. It sounded like there were people up in the attic.

All of the folks working in the department would stop what they were doing and listen, then dare each other to go have a look. There was no way anyone could have snuck up without being seen by one if not all of the people working across from the stairs.

Eventually one or two staff members would slowly make their way up the stairs and look. There was never anyone in the room that could have been making all that noise.

Paulina

Paulina was on her way to becoming a school teacher. She was attending college at the Laredo Junior College, later to become the Laredo Community College, located at the end of Washington Street.

The college is situated on what used to be Fort Macintosh, an army fort built in 1849. Some of the buildings are from the Pre-

Civil War days, others were added during World War 2.

Her father was on his way to work, and didn't want to be late, so he dropped Paulina off at the bottom of the bridge, at around 7:00 AM, near the Tutoring Center. She would walk the five blocks to her first class from there.

It was still dark at that time, but she had made this journey on several occasions and so she started off, walking to class, west to the Art's Building. This early in the morning, no one else had arrived yet, Paulina had the campus to herself, at first.

The air was still and cool, she barely made a sound as she moved over the sidewalk. As she neared the end of the street, as well as the end of the college, she saw a woman passing from Left to Right, heading to the North side of the field there.

The woman had long black hair, and was wearing a long white dress that reached the ground at, what should have been, her feet. The gown had long sleeves and was cut in an old style, perhaps from the twenties.

Being the only other person out at this hour, Paulina watched the woman as she moved. That was when she noticed, the woman didn't quite touch the ground. Her dress ended just above the ground, but there were no feet supporting her. The grass beneath her was dry and burned from the sunlight, giving it a foggy look.

The woman in white moved as if drifting, with no sign of her legs moving beneath the dress, and no disturbance of the grass she was moving over. Her hair never moved, and she paid no attention to her only witness.

Paulina didn't know what to think, they never covered this sort of thing in class. Turning she walked quickly back to the

Music Building, where a pay phone was mounted on the wall. Grabbing the phone, she called her boyfriend, who would later become her husband.

"I just saw a ghost, it was at the end of the street. What do I do?" She was shook up and still all alone.

Her boyfriend told her to; "Wait right there, don't move till other's show up."

He stayed on the phone with her until the students began to arrive for class. Once there were others around, Paulina felt safe enough to hang up and head for class.

Paulina finished her studies and became school teacher. She married her boyfriend and now has children of her own. She hopes to never see anything like that again.

S.B.P.A. Garza. Around 2006
(Supervisory Border Patrol Agent)

"We were practicing for the upcoming baseball game out at Laredo Community College. The baseball field was right next to their old cemetery. The alligator pits and the buildings weren't there yet."

"We finished up after sun down and walked out to load our gear in our cars when one of the guys stopped and just stared down the road. I turned to see what he was looking at and saw what looked like a woman, all dressed in white. She was crossing from the South to the north side of the street."

"At first she just looked like some woman, but then, I noticed her feet didn't touch the ground and she was kind of translucent."

"We all just stood there watching. No one said anything at

first, then someone asked. 'What the heck is that thing?"

"No one could say. We decided to get out of there before she came back. It was about as weird as it could get."

The "Lady in White" has not spent her entire time just haunting the campus.

All along the river banks, there are, what are called, "landings" where on occasion, people smuggling things, or people, into the country will use to get up onto the banks of the river. Just about every one of these landings has been given a name to distinguish it from all the other lands. If a large load of marijuana is caught at a particular location it might be called the "Doper's Landing." Sometimes someone will do something they wish no one knew about, like falling into the water or accidently driving a vehicle into the river. This will earn a moniker involving the agent's name.

Just up from the north wall of Fort McIntosh is a landing used by folks in the neighborhood that like to fish. Eddi "Techno" Chaves told me that on many occasions, agents have gone down to this landing only to find men and women trying to catch dinner. Thus the landing is known as the "Fisherman's Landing.

It's a nice shady place, with trees jutting out over the river giving shade to anyone standing on the bank.

Border Patrol Agents working the area will sneak down to the landing late at night to have a look for any illegal activity. The idea is to get down to the landing as quietly and without attracting the attention of the smugglers.

On many occasions the agents have slipped onto the landing and encountered the woman in white. She is seen just north or south from the Fisherman's Landing, moving through the trees as if on her way to some unknown location. The description is always the same. Long black hair down to her waist. A full length dress with long sleeves, and her feet don't touch the ground. She moves over the ground without moving any part of her body.

This has sent more than one agent running back to his unit. Once safely away they swear to never tell anyone what they've seen. No one wants to gain a reputation as seeing things.

The ghost that had been seen at the end of the street on several occasions has also been seen walking from the chapel to the gazebo on the side of the president's house. She is always described as have long black hair. A white full length dress. And she moves without touching the ground.

Who she was and why she stays close to the fort has yet to be discovered. Some believe she had been an English Teacher with some ties to the fort or the men stationed there.

With time, the opinions of others begins to lose their importance, or, the agents run into someone who is willing to listen to their stories and not pass judgement. This is how most of these stories have been passed on to be written in this book. I have talked to many Agents and Police Officers who have stories to tell but wish to remain anonymous.

7 THE ARMY MOVES ON

During the Civil War balloons were used to gain intelligence as to the positions of enemy troupes. Men would be sent aloft in baskets made from wicker to gaze down on the enemy lines using telescopes or binoculars.

On September 24, 1861, Thaddeus Lowe ascended to more than 1,000 feet in the air near Arlington, Virginia, which was across the Potomac River from Washington, DC. Once he spotted the Confederate Troupes he began telegraphing intelligence on their located at Falls Church, Virginia, which was more than three miles away. Union guns were given the range and distance then aimed and fired at the Confederate troops without ever being able to see them. This was a first in the history of warfare.

As time marched on armies continued looking for better ways to spot enemy troupe movements. When Wilber and Orville Wright launched their heavier-than-air aircraft on December 17, 1903, four miles south of Kitty Hawk, North Carolina, no one was thinking about the possible use by the military.

A few years latter Lt. Foulios was allowed to borrow a Wright Type B to ascend into the heavens and see what possible use there might be for the army. The Lieutenant was impressed. He told Washington the airplane was a viable military asset.

In February 1911, Lt. Foulios and Pioneer Pilot Philip Parmelee took off from Fort McIntosh. The pair conducted the first ever air reconnaissance along the Rio Grande River. Their mission was to look for Mexican Revolutionaries who were constantly invading towns and villages on the U.S. side of the border, as well as hostile Indian parties, and bandits.

Their route of travel took them 106 miles north west to Eagle Pass where they landed and made their report. Their flight was declared a success and Washington ordered five airplanes at a total cost of $125,000.

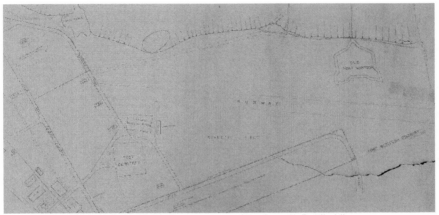
Fort McIntosh Air Field Map courtesy of the Laredo Public Library

Fort McIntosh built a runway and airplane hangars on the land just west of the cemetery. The runway ran north, passing to the east of the old Star Fort. Davalina Elementary School sits at the north end of the runway.

Some unnamed British General once said, "The airplane is useless for the purposes of war." This was a time when men still lined up and charged each other across the battle field.

As the war stretched on from 1914 both sides began using more and more aircraft. The planes had a pilot and a spotter who would look down on enemy troupes and take notes on their positions along with photographs. Should British or German planes spot each other they were limited in their ability to fight.

Some pilots carried hand guns and tried shooting at their opponents with little ability to aim. The chances of hitting a moving target from a moving plane while controlling the aircraft was beyond anyone's abilities.

The spotters began carrying rifles and then machine guns but these had to be managed by hand. Seeing this as an unwieldy means of fighting, machine guns were mounted to the aircraft but were only available for use by the spotter who was the only means of defense.

By April 1917 the use of air craft became more important to the military and President Woodrow Wilson created The U.S. Army Air Service. Their role was primarily reconnaissance.

A machine gun was mounted on the top wing of the plane allowing the pilot to fire over the top of the spinning propeller. Even though the synchronized machine gun had been invented in 1914, it wasn't all that reliable until the invention of the rotary engine. This allowed the machine gun to fire through the spinning blades without shooting down its own plane.

The dogfight was born when pilots discovered by flying straight up and then shutting off their engines they could drop back down and maneuver around their pursuers. This on and off engine created a sound like a dog barking. Ground troupes began to refer to the sound as dogs fighting, and then dogfights.

Carl was born on December 25, 1867 in Weston, Texas. He lived on the family farm along with his six siblings. His father was Reverend Joseph Rogers Darnall, a minister in the local Christian Church. His mother was Mary Ellen Thomas Darnall.

He studied at Carlton College, in Bonham, Texas, and then transferred to Transylvania University, in Lexington, Kentucky. Yes, that is the name. In 1890 he received an MD degree from

Jefferson Medical College, in Philadelphia. Dr. Darnall married Annie Estella Major, from Erwinna, Pennsylvania.

Brigadier General Carl Rogers Darnall

After a few years in the private sector, Dr. Darnall entered the United States Army receiving his commission as a Second Lieutenant in the Medical Corps.

The doctor was sent to Fort Clark, in Brackettville, Texas and then he was stationed at Fort McIntosh in Laredo. Dr. Darnall ran the hospital and treated the soldiers in Laredo for four years. His office was there in the hospital on Victoria Street. At times, he was the only doctor in the area and he would be called on to treat the folks living in Laredo as well as parts of Webb County.

In 1898 he was sent to Cuba to support the soldiers fighting the Spanish Army. Later in the war Dr. Darnall served as an operating surgeon and pathologist aboard the hospital ship USS

Relief in the Philippines and commanded the hospital at Iloilo.

In 1899 an uprising in China took place and Doctor Darnall was one of the few medical staff sent into the conflict. The uprising was known as the "Boxer Rebellion" because many of the men were practitioners of Martial Arts. The Europeans called this "Chinese Boxing." The Boxers wanted to remove all foreign influence from their country including Christian Missionaries.

In 1902, Dr. Darnall was transferred to Washington, D.C. and became an instructor of sanitary chemistry, as well as a surgeon at the Army Medical School. In 1910, Dr. Darnall invented the mechanical liquid chlorine purifier, better known as a chlorinator, used to purify drinking water. He also invented a water filter used for decades and the prototype of modern water filters used today.

During World War I, Dr. Darnall was promoted to Colonel. His talent for business and organization were recognized and he was assigned to the Finance and Supply Division in the Office of The Surgeon General.

In November, 1929, the doctor was promoted to brigadier general and became the Commanding General of the Army Medical Center, a post he held until he retired on December 31, 1931.

Darnall died on January 18, 1941 at Walter Reed General Hospital, Washington, D.C. He is buried in the Arlington National Cemetery in Arlington, Virginia.

You never know what the folks around you might do someday. A doctor stationed at Fort McIntosh went on to invent the process of chlorination that is still used today as well as help develop the water filter.

Fort McIntosh was a collection of wooden buildings and tents. There were no walls or structures designating what was army land and what was not. The main gate going into the fort was just a guard post at Victoria Street and the Railroad tracks crossing.

In 1909 an idea came up to move the fort to a new location. The current location was considered too small to accommodate a growing military presence and the fort was cut off from town by the railroad tracks. The doctor on the fort had come to the conclusion the fort's location was also a hindrance to troupes health due to its powdery soil and vicinity to the river. The land to the east of town known as "The Heights" had been chosen as the new fort location.

A land survey was done and the proposed area was staked out. The land was in the approximate area of where Bartlett and Guerrero streets are today.

The City Council met with the United States Army and held a few meetings to discuss the benefits or detriments of moving to this new location. When everything was said and done a lot more was said than done. It was decided to leave the fort where it was.

Instead of moving the fort a few improvements were undertaken. To give the troupes some off duty activity a baseball diamond was put in and bleachers built so people could watch the games without having to sit in the sun.

Having a baseball diamond led to soldiers creating their own teams. When the citizens in Laredo became interested in doing more than just watch, Laredo formed their own team to compete with the soldiers.

Then in 1910 the army decided the fort should be closed and abandoned once again. They wanted to consolidate the troupes in San Antonio and do away with distant locations.

When news reached the citizens of Laredo, Secretary Jones of the Board of Trade wrote to the Texas Senators asking them to reconsider. Senator Colberson was unavailable but Senator Bailey said he'd take it up with Washington.

The need for border protection was shown to be a real security concern and the economic impact on Laredo was also brought up. After some debate it was determined Fort McIntosh was needed to keep the United States secure so the fort was given a reprieve.

In Mexico, President Francisco Madera was in power but Mexico was still in a biter revolution. President Taft had ordered no United States Citizen should have business dealing with the Madera government. This was referred to as being the "Neutrality Law" even though the president can't make laws.

Coal Companies working along Mines Road were found to be selling coal to the Madera Government so Fort McIntosh was ordered to send a company of soldiers to guard the river to prevent coal from being shipped across the river.

The soldiers set up an outpost between the coal mines and the river which stayed in place for months.

That same year a new post exchange or PX was built to serve the troupes. This new facility held a store, barber shop, shoe repair shop, bowling alley, and a billiards room.

January 22, 1911, Captain Hagerdon, the commanding officer at the fort, sent a detail of men to find and arrest Private Andy Vicartowski. The charge was murder. The private was taken to the guardhouse and locked in a cell to await transportation.

Private Vicartowski had been known as Chas Fogel in the years before he joined the army in 1908. In 1907 Chas had been working as a brakeman for the Kansas City Railroad.

In January, Chas was visiting a "resort" in Kansas City where he was in the company of a woman. Folks in the building heard an argument coming from the room the two had been sharing. Chas stepped out into the hallway and the woman he had been with slammed the door and locked it. Chas began pounding on the door and yelling for the woman to open the door or else.

Nellie McCuine, the owner and manager of the establishment, hurried upstairs to see what all the commotion was about. She demanded Chas leave the building at once. Chas Fogel pulled a small pistol from his coat pocket and shot Nellie.

As Nellie slumped to the floor Chas ran from the building. Mary Davis was standing in the hall and watched as the man shot her boss and then ran away. Mary went to assist Nellie and wait for the authorities to arrive.

Nellie managed to hold onto life for several weeks before succumbing to her injuries. Chas Fogel was being sought for murder. He made his way to San Francisco and once there enlisted in the army using the name Andy Vicartowski, thinking there was no way the police in Kansas would be able to find him there. The army shipped Andy from one fort to another until he was stationed at Fort McIntosh in Laredo, Texas.

Mary Davis went on with her life. She Took a trip south in 1911, going to visit some friend. One day she saw a soldier walking down the street that looked familiar. After getting a better look Mary recognized the man who had killed Nellie. She contacted Police Chief Wentworth in Kansas and told him where she was and who she had seen.

Wentworth contacted Sheriff Sanchez in Webb County and made arrangements to arrest the soldier. Mary Davis was escorted to Fort McIntosh and when Private Vicartowski was brought to the guardhouse she gave a positive identification.

When Mary had pointed Chas Fogel out as being the man who killed Nellie McCuine he confessed to the murder and to using an alias in order to evade arrest.

The chances the army would sent Private Vicartowski to Fort McIntosh, in Laredo where Mary Davis had friends was incredible. Their encounter on the street was nearly too much to believe.

Men join the army for many reasons. Once they have been sworn in they sometimes discover the army was not what they had thought it might be. When you join the army you don't have the option to quit just because you're not happy doing what others tell you to do.

In 1912 Private John Crumley found himself in the army but wishing he were elsewhere. One day, he and another soldier decided it was a good idea to just pick up and leave. They took their weapons, mounted their horses and road off the fort grounds.

When the two men were discovered missing from formation they were both declared AWOL. Absent without Leave. If a war had been on, the charge would have been Desertion which held a death penalty.

Patrols that went out looking for the two men turned up only tracks heading north along the river. The pair had a head start that was impossible to close.

Customs Inspector Alex Trimble came across a pair of soldiers camped near the Rio Grande just outside a small town called Minera, twenty-two miles north of Laredo. Knowing the army was looking for two missing men he questioned them until they admitted to being away from the fort without leave.

Trimble took them into custody and escorted the pair back to Fort McIntosh. They were tried and found guilty. Both were sentenced to six years at Alcatraz Island which was a military detention facility and hadn't become a federal prison yet.

Crumley and his partner were being held in the guardhouse awaiting transport to California. While out doing what's known as "Police Call," or picking up trash, John decided he could make it to Mexico and live a free life if he could just make it to the river. He took off running, ignoring the command to halt from the sentry.

The soldier tasked with guarding the prisoners took aim and fired. The bullet hit John Crumley in the back and he fell to the ground dead, September 23, 1912. He was buried at the Fort McIntosh cemetery.

The war department decommissioned the installation on May 31, 1946 and the cemetery was closed and those interred there were either moved to the Laredo City Cemetery or Fort Sam Huston in San Antonio. John Crumley was moved to Section PE, Site 380, in San Antonio.

In 1914 the army moved the most powerful mobile radio transmitter to Fort McIntosh. It was known as a Wireless Radio because it functioned like a telegraph but did not require lines running from transmitter to receiver. The signal went out through the air in the form of Morris code. The radio transmitter was housed in the back of a truck that had been built as an ambulance but converted to electronic equipment.

The main problem with sending out wireless messages was, everyone was using the same cannel. As the operator typed out the message, it was being heard by everyone with a receiver.

The antennas were put up by a unit of eight men who were assigned to the wireless unit. The antennas stood 102 feet tall but could be set together to reach 204 feet giving the radio a farther reach. They could contact other wireless radio stations nearly a thousand miles away. The portable radio transmitter stayed at Fort McIntosh until 1917 when it was shipped to New Mexico by rail.

In its place the army began to erect a more powerful radio unit. A permanent antenna was erected just west of the hospital and a building was constructed where the wireless equipment could be set up.

The new wireless radio could reach other stations several thousand miles away. Since all military transmissions went out over the same frequency, the radio would only transmit twice a day. Once from 9:15 until 10:15 AM and then from 1:15 until 2:15 PM. The rest of the time the radiomen were to listen for other transmitters. Should a situation arise needing to be broadcast, the radio operators could send out emergency transmissions any time.

The huge tower was made from steel trusses with a ladder running up the side for maintenance of the antenna. Guy wires ran out to make the tower secure during an storms that might arise.

On March 14, 1915, Pvt. William Banks, Troupe I of the 14th Cavalry was in town visiting a woman he knew. He had arrived around 9:30 P.M. The place was known as being a "Questionable Resort" also known as a brothel.

At 9:40, Corporal Everett McCoy arrived and insisted Banks accompany him outside. He had a pistol on his belt. The two soldiers went outside and an argument could be heard. This was followed by a shot. When the people in the house finally looked outside, Pvt. Banks was dead with a gunshot to the chest.

Corporal McCoy ran for the border. He began hanging out at various bars in town and when men from the fort would cross into Mexico for a week-end, they reported seeing him as the corporal slipped away into the darkness. He was described as being near falling down drunk anytime he was seen.

On March 17, a patrol of soldiers were camped out in San Ygnacio, forty miles south from Laredo. A disheveled figure approached them and reported to the sergeant in charge. Corporal McCoy had decided to turn himself in.

The corporal had swum the river south of town and spent the night sleeping in the brush. He was taken into custody and transported back to Fort McIntosh. Since the original crime had taken place in town, McCoy was turned over to the Laredo Police who took him to the county jail.

Corporal McCoy was stripped of his rank. He was then tried for murder. During the trial it became apparent McCoy and Banks were both "involved" with the same woman. Even though the woman was being paid to be romantically involved with many men, McCoy had developed strong feelings for her and decided she should only be involved with him. McCoy had acted on the spur of the moment and killed his rival. He was found guilty of manslaughter and sentenced to five years in the state prison.

Private Banks' body was shipped back to his home town.

On May 1, 1915, the Lusitania departed New York City bound for Liverpool. What most folks didn't know, including her passengers, almost all her cargo consisted of munitions and contraband destined for the British war effort. It was illegal for any neutral country to supply arms or ammunition to any hostile countries during a time of war. The Germans did know what was being transported in the hold because of spies along the waterfront.

On May 7, 1915, Lusitania was passing Ireland when Lt. Walther Schwieger, Captain of the U-20 spotted the liner. Knowing it was filled with munitions he fired one torpedo. It hit on the starboard or right side near the bow. The torpedo hit was followed by an explosion. Suddenly there was an enormous detonation and the ship began to sink.

Walther Schwieger was a Lieutenant in the Kriegsmarine and he was the Captain of the U-Boat. His official title was Lieutenant Captain.

Due to the ship leaning far over to one side only six of the forty-eight life boats could be lowered. One thousand, one hundred and ninety-eight people died as a result. Of these, one hundred and twenty-eight were Americans.

Many believe this was the spark that brought the United States into the War in Europe but it was only one small item that eventually lead to war.

The Plan de San Diego was being spread amongst the Spanish speaking residents of Webb County. The plan said the Mexican Military was going to invade Texas and reclaim it for Mexico. All white residents would be imprisoned or shot. The state was to be divided up and land was to be given to blacks and Indians who lived in the area. People were all talking about the coming invasion and many folks packed their belongings and moved away hoping to avoid the bloodshed.

Due to the fighting in Mexico, many refugees were marching

north hoping to seek asylum in the United States. As many as 5000 people were in the group. Soldiers from Fort McIntosh were sent out to stop these refuges at the border. The folks making up the asylum seekers were unemployed or extremely low income street dwellers who had no money or families living along the border to take them in. They were going to throw themselves on the good will of the United States.

Once they arrived in Nuevo Laredo, the refugees discovered they would not be allowed into the US and the folks living in Nuevo Laredo didn't want them either. They slowly vanished back into the interior.

Radio stations in Mexico began contacting ranches along the border speaking only in Spanish and asking the workers to rise up and overthrow the government. This overthrow would be supported by the Mexican Army which was "on its way" to invade Texas. Bandits, many in the Mexican Army, began attacking outlying ranches along the border.

Fearing the report of a coming invasion might be true many ranchers began flying a German flag to try appearing as if they were German descendants. Surprisingly this worked in many locations since the bandits avoided attacking these ranches. The Mexican Army was filled with German Officers that had suddenly immigrated in the last few months. These bandits didn't want to upset their commanding officers.

A newspaper in Laredo, "El Progreso," a local Spanish only paper, was printing news articles about the coming invasion. This stirred up the worries of those who received their news from just this one source. The paper began asking the locals to "Reassess their loyalties to Mexico."

The soldiers at Fort McIntosh were placed on alert thinking there just might be something to all these stories. The commander notifies Washington he believed there may be as many as 500 well-armed rebels in Laredo waiting for their chance to attack.

In a bid to stop all these rumors and bring peace to Laredo, a group of "Concerned Citizens" walked into the editors office of El Progreso and removed him at gun point. The editor, who was actually a white guy, was taken to a low water crossing north of Fort McIntosh and told to cross into Mexico and never come back, or else. They then returned to the newspaper office, sent all the worker home, and locked the building. The newspaper was actually owned by the Carranza Government in Mexico.

The Mexican Ambassador complained to Washington about the treatment of this US citizen. Washington contacted the Texas Governor and asked him to look into this situation. The governor contacted the Webb County District Attorney to find out if this story was true. The District Attorney told Austin that yes the story was true but the people involved were all amongst the upper class citizens of Laredo. The matter was dropped.

All along the border, fights broke out between longtime residents and those recently arrived. No one knew who lived in Texas and who might be a bandit. In Laredo, this wasn't a problem. Once El Progreso stopped printing stories to drive a wedge between the rich and poor, things got back to normal. Or as close as possible during these times.

It turned out, the Plan de San Diego was all a construction of the German Military. They had come up with this in a bid to start a war between Mexico and the United States to keep the U.S. out of the European Conflict. The Carranza Government was hesitant to attack their neighbors to the north. Carranza was afraid any move on his part would invite another invasion into his country.

In 1916, rumors of a Mexican Invasion began to circulate

throughout the border region once again. It was said General Carranza was sending an army into Nuevo Laredo with the intention of crossing into Laredo and attacking the United States. This time the reports were backed by the movement of Mexican military units enroute to Nuevo Laredo. The commander at Fort McIntosh believed this time Mexico was intent on destroying Laredo.

As these reports spread across the country, troupes were shipped to forts along the border. Militia units and volunteers began to arrive along the border as well. The militia was welcomed in as a part of the military buildup. The volunteers were encouraged to enlist. Carranza was told about the sudden increase in military units in every location north of the Rio Grande. He thought the United States was preparing to invade his country so he backed off from his plan. The Mexican Army was moved back to the interior. Once it was discovered this latest attack was overblown, the troupes were told it was time to get on with training. They would be needing it soon.

Troupes were stationed at forts all along the border between the United States and Mexico. When word would reach the commanding officers of incursions within their jurisdictions they would send out men to look for the people entering the country illegally. Time would be lost as the troupes made their way from the forts to the areas where the suspicious activity had occurred.

In 1916 it was decided to cut down on response time, men should be placed in locations in between the forts so they would be closer to where they might need to be. Instead of having them sitting in camp waiting for orders, the men would actively patrol the river. The men at Fort McIntosh were amongst the first to take part in this ongoing patrol of the border.

Troup K, 14th Cavalry set out early in the morning riding north to the St. Tomas coal fields. They would be setting up their outpost near the Town of Dolores. Not to be confused with the Dolores Mission which was south from Laredo.

Once in the small town the troupes gathered their equipment from the railroad station and then moved to a clear area closer to the river. The troupes set up tents and laid in a supply of wood for cooking. Then they set out to scout the area and familiarize themselves with the terrane.

The setting up of outposts in the areas between the forts became a regular activity between Brownsville and El Paso, Texas. The soldiers would spend up to a month away from the barracks. Food and other supplies had to be brought along or scavenged from the surrounding brush.

The Rio Grande and Eagle Pass rail line used to head up along the river to haul coal into Laredo. From 1889 until 1942 this rail line was in operation. A small section continued to operate to service the Laredo Flexible Gunnery School at Laredo Air Base near milepost 7 which was continued until 1947.

Luis F Bean of the New Hampshire National Guard arrived At Fort McIntosh. The Plan de San Diego had caused quite a stir in Washington and troupes were sent south to help guard the border.

In order to accommodate this massive influx of manpower, tents were set up in any location not already occupied by buildings. Each gathering of tents was given a name such as "Camp Missouri" or "Camp New Hampshire." The men would be assigned to either guard duties or patrolling the river. Those guarding the bridge from Laredo to Nuevo Laredo were told no one was to cross the bridge without showing a proper pass. The threat of Carransistas, troupes under Carranza, sneaking into Laredo was very real.

In November, at 6 AM, Private Bean was about to be relived

at the International bridge. His relief arrived and they exchanged pleasantries. As they stood there in the early morning light, two men began crossing the bridge from Mexico.

The two soldiers noticed each man walking towards them was holding a coat rolled up and held tight under their arms. The soldiers ordered the men to halt and show what they were secreting in their coats. When the two men refused shots were fired and the two men were both killed.

What they had hidden in their coats was never revealed. The men had fallen on the Mexican side of the bridge. Soldiers came from Nuevo Laredo, picked up the two bodies and their bundles and took them south.

Private Bean was allowed to return to the fort after a cursory investigation. His orders had been clear, no one was to cross without a proper pass. The reports of this incident are lost somewhere in the old records from 1916. Private Bean had written letters home on a regular bases and this was the only written record of the shooting.

A few nights later, Bean was awoken in the middle of the night by calls to action. Jumping from his bunk, he pulled on his boots having slept in his uniform.

Once outside, he was told men had snuck into the fort and were attempting to steal horses and mules. The soldiers grabbed their rifles and began firing at the retreating shapes that were running for the river.

Once the shooting had stopped no invaders were found. The escaping men had taken the wounded with them.

A few weeks after the assault on the corals, Private Bean and his unit were sent to Zapata to set up an outpost. The men were to march the 63 miles. When they arrived in San Ygnacio, they spotted four white crosses marking the location where the soldiers had died during the attack from Mexico.

It took them four and a half day to march from Laredo to Zapata. When they arrived the men setup their camp in the area around the county court house and the post office. Trenches were dug between the tents and the river. These were reinforced with wood and rocks. As night fell, guards would be stationed in the trenches to watch for hostile activity along the river.

Falcon Lake wouldn't be created until 1950.

Late at night, shots would be fired from Mexico into the United States. The guards would blow a whistle to alert the rest of the soldiers who would run to man the trenches. Bullets would fly back and forth but there is no record of anyone ever actually being shot. Many of the civilians living nearby would run to help man the trenches. Women and children in the area would run and take shelter in either the court house or post office since both buildings were made from brick.

In November, 1916 men were stationed at Fort McIntosh waiting for the "Big Push" to begin. The Lusitania was just one small spark to get the US into the war but it took a while to fan the flames. When the Zimmerman telegram was revealed the folks in the US decided it was time to act. Everyone was talking about how it wouldn't be long before the United States got involved in the European Conflict and then the Kaiser would see who was boss.

Soldiers were patrolling the border looking for bandits who were crossing the river and attacking U.S. citizens. Soldiers of Troop K, of the 14th Cavalry unit were back at the fort, out in the stables preparing their mounts. Pvt. Jones, Pvt. McKnight,

and Pvt. Conners, were tending to the horses when Corporal
William Smith walked into their area. He drew his side arm and
began to fire from point blank range. Pvt. Jones and Pvt.
McKnight were both hit in the center of their chests, killing
them outright as the bullets passed through their hearts. Pvt.
Conners was hit in the shoulder, falling to the ground, shocked
by this unprovoked attack.

Corporal Smith kept firing his revolver until he had expended
all the rounds in the cylinder. This gave the others in Troop K
an opining to jump him and wrestle the weapon from his grip.

Pvt. Conners was taken to the post hospital and received
treatment for his wound.

The corporal was hustled away to the guard house, which was
only a block away, and placed in a cell for safe keeping. He was
charged with two murders as well as a assault to commit a third.
During questioning, it was learned Smith had become addicted
to heroin at some point in his career. The night before going on
his rampage he couldn't get ahold of any of his much needed
drugs and this caused him to go berserk. Smith decided he was
going to kill five soldiers and then himself. His mental state was
blamed on his use of drugs.

The next morning U.S. Marshal Walker arrived at the fort,
took custody of Corporal Smith and placed him in the Webb
County Jail to await trial. During questioning the corporal didn't
seem the least bit upset that he had just killed two of his fellow
soldiers and wounded a third. Smith was under the impression
he had killed all three of the men he had shot. His actions made
the investigators believe the man was not in his right mind. The
authorities decided to have Smith examined by professionals.

Corporal Smith was shipped to Galveston and placed in a
psychiatric hospital. After two months of observation by
Alienists, psychiatrists trained in determining a person's mental
state before going to trial, Smith was determined to be incapable

of standing trial. He was then sent back to Fort McIntosh.

The military declared Smith to be "Mentally Aberrated" and sent him to an asylum for "treatment" until he either recovered or was no longer a threat. There is no record of his ever being released.

Bayer Drug Company began manufacturing diacetylmorphine in 1895 and marketed it under the name Heroin. It was then widely distributed and available in over-the-counter form. You could buy heroin for just about any medical problem, from a headache to depression. By 1924 approximately 200,000 people in the United States had become addicted to heroin. The United States Congress banned the manufacture, sale and importation of this drug.

Later, the same day as the shooting on the fort, a soldier, Pvt. Paul Tory was hit by a passing train in the late hours of the evening but his body wasn't found until the morning of the next day. In order to leave or enter the fort soldiers had to cross the railroad tracks which were not lit and the crossings were dangerous even in the day time.

Pvt. Michael Headin was walking along the street of the fort when he fell forward onto his chest. He had been holding tin cup and the metal was driven into his body. The private then drug himself a short ways along the dirt road until he died from his injuries. There was no indication as to why he had fallen.

Four men all died the same day and one was seriously wounded.

This same month Zimmerman became the German Foreign Minister. He sent a telegram to Van Eckhardt, Germanys

Ambassador in Mexico City, asking the Mexican Government to ally itself with Japan and then invade the United States. Japan decided it was best to take sides with the British and French. German then asked Mexico City to join Germany and attack the United States. The Carranza Government declined this offer.

What the Germans didn't know was, British Intelligence had broken their codes and now had the full details of the German offer to Mexico. British Intelligence passed this document onto the United States.

On December 3, 1916 men had been given leave to unwind in town. There were two movie theaters in town and some men went to watch their entertainment instead of drinking it.

In the middle of the movies a message was flashed on the screens. "All Personnel Are To Report To Fort." There was a mass exodus as soldiers went looking for transportation back to their units.

A phone call had come in from a rancher saying he had spotted a large number of suspicious looking men on the Mexican side of the river.

Sixty-four members of the Motorcycle Machine Gun Company road out and sped to the location of what might be a buildup for invasion.

Once they arrived at the ranch, the men set up a perimeter to wait for the next move. The night ran its course and the next morning the soldiers returned to the fort. The men in Mexico appeared to have been camped out and had moved on when the sun was up.

The fort was home to many different units. There were Field Artillery, Coastal Artillery, they had much bigger cannon, Infantry, Cavalry, Engineers, the Signal Corps, and a Truck Company. All were soldiers who had specialized ways of doing their jobs. Horses, motorcycles, trucks, cannon, and radio equipment all there to protect the United States.

A building set up at Camp Missouri, the northern part of the fort, was dismantled and moved to the main part of the fort to be used as a YMCA. The YMCA handled many of the day to day activities the men were used to from when they were not in the army. Things like supplying toiletries and handling the mail. They also provided after hours activities for the men not assigned to guard, or other military duties.

In April, 1917, two and a half years after the start of World War I the United States declared war on Germany using the sinking of the Lusitania by a German U-Boat as just cause. Germany was still holding on to the belief that Mexico would side with them in a bid to regain Texas. The German, Mexican alliance never took place.

The telegram Zimmerman had sent to Mexico is believed by some, to have had more impact on the decision to declare war than the sinking of the Lusitania. Lusitania may have been used publicly to keep the braking of the German code by British Intelligence secret.

Men needed to be trained to fight and many began their first month in the army stationed at Fort McIntosh. Evan in the 1900s the army was still training on horseback. Men would be trained on how to ride into battle, dismount and engaged the enemy. In the opening days of war this was utilized in France and Belgium but as soon as the trenches were dug, horses were there to pull cannon and wagons. The days of the mounted charge were in the past.

The army was always looking for better means of doing things. Not everything was frozen in the past. In 1917 the army sent out a bunch of bulldozers pulling trains of wagons, some as many as fifteen hooked together, from Fort Sam Houston in San Antonio, 150 miles south to Fort McIntosh in Laredo. The average speed was 3 MPH. Think about that the next time you taking a long trip. Each wagon in the train was filled to capacity. The roads between the two forts were not in very good shape. This was a test to see if different forms of transport could be used on the battle field. The Bulldozer Train was declared a success.

There were few buildings at Fort McIntosh
so the men lived in tents.
Postcards compliments of Laredo Public Library

At Fort McIntosh, the 37th Infantry were being trained for battle

In 1917 the roads in the United States were not designed for mass vehicle traffic. Some roads were just dirt. A convoy of vehicle might average 5 miles per hour over a long distance maneuver. Most roads in that time were far weather only and became impassable in rain or snow.

There were many German National in the United States. Thinking Mexico might join Germany in the war against the U.S. these German citizens all began making their way to the southern border. These folks tended to stick out in a crowd due to their mannerisms and speech. Any time anyone suspected of being from Germany was encountered, the authorities would be called. Many of these foreign nationals wound up being held at Fort McIntosh. Once facilities had been set up at Fort Douglas in Utah, the prisoners were transferred by rail.

Two Germans being held at Fort McIntosh were paroled from the guardhouse with the understanding they were not to leave Laredo.

The two men, Heinrich Schmidt and Johan Schmidt, with the same last name but not related, began walking north from the fort. When they were near the Indian Crossing they both ran towards the river.

Mounted Inspector Corwin spotted the two and went to arrest them. Heinrich dove into the river and was able to swim into Mexico. Johan was taken into custody and returned to the fort. His parole was terminated and he spent the next few months waiting for transport to Fort Douglas.

In October, 1917 a group of seven German POWs tunneled from their jail cell at Fort McPherson in Georgia. They wanted to escape from the United States but didn't have a real good idea as to where the U.S. Mexican border was easiest to cross. They worked their way west and then south winding up in Texas.

Two of the escapees, Captain Hans Berg and Lieutenant Alfred Leoscher entered Laredo looking for the easiest way to cross into Mexico.

They were in town for about a week before deciding to try crossing farther south from town. The pair wound up spotting a fisherman on the Mexico side of the river five miles from town. As they attempted to communicate with the man on the other side of the river a pair of men road up on horseback.

The two Germans thought these were just a pair of cowboys and told them they were from Germany and were trying to escape from the country.

Unbeknownst to them the two men on horses were Robert Ramsey and John Chamberlain, U.S. Mounted Inspectors. The inspectors took the two Germans into custody and transported them to Fort McIntosh.

The Customs Service had been using mounted customs inspectors who patrolled the northern and southern borders since 1853. The "Chinese Exclusion Act" enacted in 1882 was difficult to enforce so the Bureau of Immigration developed Mounted Immigration Guards along the borders in 1915 often referred to as Mounted Inspectors. When Prohibition was enacted in 1920, the strain on Bureau of Immigration's resources became too much to handle. The U.S. Immigration Border Patrol was formed in 1924 to patrol the border and enforce both Prohibition and the Chinese Immigration Act.

Once at the fort the two re-incarcerated men told the soldiers they didn't know where the rest of the escapees were. They had separated during their trip to Texas, with the other Germans heading south instead of south west.

These two men had served aboard the German Auxiliary Cruiser Mowe, which means seagull. This ship had sunk or captured forty-five British and French ships.

The Germans were placed in the guardhouse to await transport to another POW camp. It would be several weeks before the two Germans could be transported back to Georgia. Orders came through on November 11 for the two men to be taken by train back to Fort McPherson.

A jail break took place at Fort McIntosh when Corporal Otto Miller, of the 14th Cavalry, helped Paul Ruthling sneak out of his cell and escape into the night. Ruthling had been arrested for helping four Austrian and one German prisoner escape earlier that week. These men were being held having been accused of spying on the United States. Two of the Austrians had drown in the river trying to escape to Mexico. The others are believed to have made it.

Otto Miller and Ruthling were seen sitting in the plaza in

Nuevo Laredo for the next several days. Soldiers crossing into Nuevo Laredo for the day would see the two men sitting on a bench or sometimes walking about the plaza. Once back at the fort they would report what they had seen.

Official requests were sent to the Mexican Government for the return of the deserter and suspected spy but nothing was ever done about them.

As you can see, the ties to heritage sometimes outweighs the ties to their new homes.

Prostitution has followed the military since men began carrying arms. Laws have been passed trying to do away with these "Ladies of Negotiable Affections" as Terry Pratchett liked to call them.

In 1917 it was illegal to have a house of prostitution within five miles of any fort within the United States. During World War I, the U.S. Government developed a public health program called the "American Plan" which authorized the military to arrest any woman within five miles of a military fort or camp who worked as a prostitute.

Military Police, Laredo Police, and U.S. Marshals worked together making raids on locations where prostitutes and gambling were believed to be operating. Any troupes found in one of these locations would be arrested and taken to the Guardhouses on the fort. Some of the women, regardless of the citizenship, were also taken to Fort McIntosh and placed in an Immigration Camp located on the north end of the fort. Once in the Immigration Camp the women would have to wait for their day in court to discover their future.

Men from all walks of life joined the military to serve their countries. Even Bela Lugosi, the man who would later portray "Dracula" in movies joined the Austrian Army. Men joined the army here in Laredo and went away to do what they hoped was the right thing. Many of them died in foreign lands, their bodies never being found.

David Barkley was born in Laredo, Texas on March 31, 1899. His father, Joseph S. Barkley, was a career soldier who was stationed at Fort McIntosh. After David was born, Joseph was relocated to Puerto Rico. Antonia Cantu, David's mother, stayed in Texas along with their two children.

David enlisted in the Texas National Guard. When the United States entered World War I, David enlisted in the Army. Private David B. Barkley Cantu was stationed at Fort Ringgold in Rio Grande City, before being shipped over to France. He was a Private in the 155th Infantry when the unit arrived in France in August, 1918. After serving at the front for a few months, Private Berkley was reassigned to Company A, 356th Infantry Regiment, 89th Division.

The war was drawing to a close when Private Berkley, and Sergeant Waldo Hatler, were given the task of crossing the Meuse River to reconnoiter the enemy and find out their troupe strength and locations.

This was not an easy assignment. Soldiers would remove anything that might make noise from their uniforms. They would have to sneak into the enemies lines and then move from place to place in total darkness trying to spy on the people who wanted to kill them. A rifle would only weigh them down and might make noise so the only weapons they would carry were trench knives and a pistol. If things went wrong the pair would be lucky if they were caught and taken prisoner. More than likely they would simply be shot.

This was November in France. The air was cold and the water even colder. The two soldiers managed to swim across the river without being spotted by German snipers. Now, in wet clothing, they moved about in the dark looking for the enemy. After scouting out the German positions, the two soldiers made their way back to the river. Just a few more minutes and they could get out of these freezing cold, water soaked uniforms, and into something dry and warm.

They reentered the river and began to swim. Private Berkley felt his muscles begin to cramp. Had he cried out for the sergeant to give him a hand he would have drawn the attention of the German snippers who were stationed all along the front.

David Berkley was unable to make the swim. He drown on November 9, 1918, just two days before the Armistice on the eleventh hour of the eleventh day of the eleventh month, 1918.

Private Barkley is one of only three Texans to be awarded the Medal of Honor during World War I. Additionally, France awarded him the Croix de Guerre, and Italy the Croce al Merito di Guerra.

Private Barkley lay in state at the Alamo, the second person to ever receive this honor. He was then buried at the San Antonio National Cemetery. The Chapel at Fort McIntosh was later named for Private David Berkley.

George Bigden was in high school in Laredo when the Civil War broke out in Mexico. He joined the Army National Guard and was stationed at Fort McIntosh, assigned to patrolling the border until 1917.

When the United States officially entered the European

Conflict thus turning it into a World War, George was transferred to the U.S. Army.

George showed a natural ability for leadership and was promoted to Corporal in early 1918. He started out being assigned to the "Lone Star Division," a division made up almost completely of men from Texas. He was assigned to B company, 141st Infantry, 36th Division once he and his fellow soldiers were in France. By the middle of 1918, George had become a Sergeant.

On the morning of October 8, 1918, the men were told to prepare for an assault on the German lines. Both sides were entrenched along a wandering line that ran from the border of Switzerland all the way to the English Channel.

For years both sides had dug in and fortified their positions. The only way to get either side out of their trenches was to run across "Noman's Land" and force them out.

At the given time, a whistle was blown giving the signal it was time to attack. George clomb the ladder from the trench and began the long run, leading the men under him towards the enemy. He never made it to the German lines. A bullet had found him and he fell to the ground.

His body was later recovered and shipped back to the United States for burial.

On June 10, 1919, Sergeant Bigden was awarded the Croix de Guerre by the French government. The Croix de Guerre may either be awarded as an individual or unit award to those soldiers who distinguish themselves by acts of heroism involving combat with the enemy.

George died on October 8, 1918. At the same time, on the

same day, in Texas, on the other side of the world, Jack Beverly Bigden was born.

Jack Beverly Bigden joined the Marine Corps and was sent to fight in Korea. He was assigned to F Company of the 7th Division and soon promoted to Sergeant while serving his country. He died in battle on November 3, 1950.

The Grave Marker for George was provided by Michael Randy Walsh.
The Grave Marker for Jack was provided by Ann Cody.
They are both buried at Arlington National Cemetery.

Both of these men had the same last name and rose to the same rank and both died fighting for their country. As one was dying the other was being born. They were both from Texas.

On September 7, 1919 Lieutenant Van Johnson readied his plane at the Fort McIntosh Airfield. He was to patrol north from Laredo along with his passenger, Captain Davis McNabb. The captain was in charge of the 2nd Flight, 8th Aero Squadron.

The two men were to fly along the river looking for any sign of bandits trying to enter the United States. They took off at around 9:00 AM and followed the river. As they were closing on Santa Isabel Creek, 16 miles from the fort, they spotted a group of horses on the Mexican side of the river. The horses were saddled and ready for use.

Lt. Johnson took the plane down low so the captain could get a better look. As the plane was level with the horses, shots rang out. Someone was firing at the plane from the other side of the river. The captain was hit in the head as the pilot pulled back on the stick and tried to take evasive maneuvers.

The pilot couldn't fly the plane and treat his captain at the same time so he looked for a field where he could land. The best place he could see was the Leyendecker Farm.

As the plane set down in the field the workers ran to assist. The captain was taken from the rear seat of the biplane and carried into the main house. His injury was examined by one of the women who discovered the bullet had hit just below the left ear but didn't look as if it had broken the skull.

The Leyendecker farm was a big property and they had a phone so word was sent to the fort telling of the injured captain.

At Fort McIntosh a second plane was dispatched with the doctor onboard. The plane flew to the Leyendecker Farm and landed so the doctor could examine the patient. He found the woman had been right, the bullet had damaged the skin but didn't break the skull. An ambulance arrived shortly and the captain was loaded up and taken back to the fort hospital.

Captain McNabb was stitched up and allowed to recover as the investigation into what had happened began.

The General in charge of the garrison in Nuevo Laredo was driven out to the area across from Santa Isabel Creek where he interviewed the men there. This was a company of soldiers from the Mexican Army. The men all said the airplane was flying over

Mexico and they shot at it because it was scaring their horses.

The General sent an Official Complaint to Fort McIntosh accusing Lt. Johnson and Captain McNabb of entering Mexico illegally.

The inquest from San Antonio interviewed men who had been working near Santa Isabel Creek. Over fifty men all stated the plane was not over Mexico but was over the US when the shooting took place.

When the evidence had all been gathered it appeared as if the soldiers in Mexico had fired on the plane even though it was on the other side of the river. The Carranza Government in Mexico City sent an apology for shooting at an American Airplane.

This was not the first or last time soldiers from Mexico were involved in altercations on the United States side of the border. In October, Clemente Vergara and Porfirio Laura were both killed by Mexican soldiers while in the United States. Many of the bandits caught crossing the river turned out to be soldiers.

From 1917 to 1918 15,000 recruits pass through the gates of Fort McIntosh for training, many of them were sent to France or Belgium to fight in the trenches.

On March 11, 1918 the company cook at Camp Funston which was a post at Fort Riley, Kansas, reported to Sick-Call with a headache nausea, low grade fever, and muscle aches. Sergeant Albert Mitchell was sent to his barracks and told to stay there for the next day or so. By the next morning there were 107 soldiers, all complaining of the same symptoms.

Soldiers being trained to ride into battle on horseback.
Photograph courtesy of National Archives.

At the time no one thought this was anything other than a case of the flu. The war was still on and men got sick. This was considered normal. The men were given the same orders and aspirin was handed out by the hands full.

By the following morning, the Sick-Call list was up to 522 men and many more should have reported but had decided to tough it out.

The Fort commanders began to suspect there might be foul play. Maybe some German spy had managed to slip some unknown poison into the food supply.

The first thing to happen was a complete blackout of all news reports. The soldiers should be back on their feet in no time now that they were being treated. The town next door was searched for any suspicious looking individuals. Security was stepped up at the gates going in and out.

The war was still on and soldiers were needed at the front so trains ran on schedule and soldiers moved out from Fort Riley to other parts of the country. Any soldiers feeling sick were held back until the "poison" was out of their systems.

Soldiers arrived at their new duty station only to report to Sick-Call. They had begun to feel sick shortly after arriving. The company doctors suspected war nerves or maybe just travel sickness or even these soldiers were slackers who didn't want to serve their country.

Then civilians began to get sick. With the total news blackout, no one connected the dots. Had anyone been able to watch the spread of this illness they would have noticed it spread outwards from Fort Riley along the rail lines to other parts of the country.

Soldiers shipped across the Atlantic were showing signs of this flu like disease. The hospitals at an army camp in Bordeaux, France, and in the port city of Brest began to fill with sick men. As men moved about the battle fields those in the trenches began to fall ill as well.

The news about what had become a worldwide epidemic was still being controlled as national security. England, France, and The United States all kept a lid on what was going on not wanting the enemy to know just how bad things were getting. Spain had declared themselves neutral during the war. The newspapers had no qualms about reporting what was going on. Once news had spread from Spain back to the United States, people began to refer to the outbreak as being the "Spanish Flu."

Anytime soldiers surrendered or were captured they would be held in POW camps. This cost money and took men away from fighting in order to guard the enemy prisoners. It was common practice to swop prisoners from one side to the other. As German troupes were returned to their country they carried the flu with them. It wasn't long before the illness was in the German trenches as well.

In August, 1918, a new strain of the flu cropped up. It was first reported in France, Sierra Leon, and the United States. People would become sick and die even with the most advance treatments. The mortality rate ran as high as fifty present of those who contracted the Spanish Flu.

In October, 1918, 23 year old Private William Byer reported to the hospital at Fort McIntosh. He was soon joined by 51 other soldiers. The hospital was soon over crowded with men all complaining of the same symptoms. Headache, nausea, muscle aches, and a low fever. Doctors did the only thing they could think of. Hand out aspirin and keep the men in bed. A quarantine was in effect but it was too late. When the flu virus first enters the body the person feels okay. They become contagious by the next day and may still be infectious up to two weeks later. They begin to feel sick long after spreading the disease all over their surroundings.

With a mortality rate of over one third, the number of dead at Fort McIntosh may have reached at least seventeen men. The numbers were held under national security so we may never know how many actually died during the 1918-1919 outbreak.

Laredo and the surrounding area had a surprisingly mild run during the second outbreak. Few people became sick unlike other large military towns. It may have been due to the policy of quarantining any new troupes arriving at Fort McIntosh.

Troupes arriving from other forts or camps went straight to a holding center until they had been on the fort for two weeks. There were two-thousand, five-hundred men in the center at one time. At the end of this forced separation they were released to join the rest of the companies.

Fort McIntosh wasn't the only military establishment to use quarantining but it worked for the Laredo area.

By the end of the outbreak, as many as one hundred million people may have died from the Spanish Flu. About three hundred people died in Laredo.

Mr. G.

G was a student at Laredo Community College back in 2014. He was doing work studies at the Media Center next door to the College President's House.

Like a lot of students Mr. G didn't have a car so he had to rely on others to get transport to college. One morning his father had dropped him off at 6:00 AM and then drove away to work. G discovered the doors to the center were all locked so he began walking around just to do something.

His route of travel took him north to Tayler Street and the Army Reserve Center. From there G began walking east past the old stone building built in 1943.

As he was walking he began to feel as if there was someone right behind him. Turning to see who was there, G saw he was alone. Turning back east, G walked along the sidewalk slowly getting the feeling he was now surrounded by others. It felt like he was in a formation of marching men.

Having been in the ROTC for years, G felt himself in formation marching along with a squad of unseen men. He could hear and feel their feet pounding the ground. He could feel the energy as the men marched to an unseen commander.

A "facing maneuver" was announced, unheard but obeyed just the same "Rear March!" G made an about face and marched back west wondering why he was following these commands. "Why did I do that?" He asked himself. As he grew farther from the reserve center the feeling of the group began to fade. By 6:30, G found himself walking back to the Media Center by himself.

After thinking about that day for several weeks G decided to ask around to see if anyone had ever reported any kind of similar occurrence. He approached his Kinesiology Professor and broached the subject of odd feelings or occurrences.

The professor said, back in about 1998 or 2000 there had been a weird incident involving the softball team.

The team was about to begin practice at around sundown. They walked onto the diamond and began throwing the ball back and forth to warm up. One of the players turned to face the cemetery and saw something hanging from a tree. Just outside the cemetery wall was a body hanging in the air.

He yelled for his fellow ballplayers and began running to the tree, thinking a suicide had just occurred. The ball players all ran to help the person, as one of the players tried to dial 911 to get an ambulance enroute.

The ball players arrived at the tree to find the body was gone. They turned in circles trying to figure out how they might have run past the body in such a hurry to help. Several of them looked in the bushes trying to see if just maybe the body had fallen to the ground.

The guy with the cell phone stopped trying to call when he

realized there was confusion as to whether someone was dying or not.

The mad dash to help turned into a confused walk as the ball players looked around trying to figure out what had been mistaken for a body hanging from a tree. It's not that far from where they had seen it to where they were now searching.

As the realization set in it was decided to keep this incident to themselves. No one wanted to say they had seen something that wasn't there.

Mr. G is studying history with hopes of becoming a Military Historian.

The Civil Air Patrol was conceived in the late 1930s by aviation advocate Gill Robb Wilson, who foresaw general aviation's potential to supplement America's military operations. In 1936 Gill Wilson had just returned from Germany. He was convinced the country was preparing for war. With the help of New York Mayor LaGuardia, in his capacity as then-Director of the Office of Civilian Defense. CAP was created on December 1, 1941. Texas oilman David Harold Byrd was a co-founder of Civil Air Patrol.

The Civil Air Patrol flew out of Fort McIntosh.

This same year the subject of moving Fort McIntosh came up once more. The Laredo Chamber of Commerce along with the Command Staff of the fort took the train north to Form Sam Houston where they met with Major General Parker, the commanding officer of the 8th Corps.

Once more the problem of the fort being too small to support a battalion, and it being cut off by the railroad tracks came up. Should there be a north bound train there was no way to get into or out of the fort and into Laredo. When all the options were gone over it was decided to leave the fort where it was.

8 THE LITTLE GIRL

The idea of a small child dying and its ghost lingering on long after their passing is probably one of the worst ideas when it comes to paranormal. Kids aren't supposed to have unfinished business. They're not supposed to have done anything to warrant their staying on in this plane of existence.

At Fort McIntosh, people have seen a little girl hanging around at several locations. The image they report is a girl, about seven or eight years old. She's dressed in old style clothing. Her shoes have button along the sides. This would put her as having lived around 1870 to 1914.

People see a young girl walking along the sidewalk or crossing the streets on the fort. Then they lose sight of her and simply write it off thinking she must have turned a corner or entered one of the buildings. It's not unheard of for a young girl to enter one of the campus structures. Her odd dress is just a mistake in viewing. Most of these sightings never get mentioned.

A police officer was checking out a report of suspicious activity at the motor pool late one night. This area was west from the Guardhouse, behind the old book store.

The officer spotted someone walking around in the yard where vehicles were stored. He could see it was a young girl who shouldn't have been wandering about so late at night. There is a neighborhood just a few hundred yards south from the yard. People lived there along with many small children. Maybe she had wandered away from her home? Perhaps she's playing some kind of game?

The Officer asked her what she was doing wandering around in an area off limits to unauthorized personal. The girl just kept walking along as if she hadn't hear him. He was about to follow when the little girl faded from view. One second she was there, looking as real as anyone. She was gone so quick the officer thought she must have ducked down behind something.

He walked over with his flashlight and looked behind and under the vehicles. The yard wasn't that full to begin with. As he was looking he realized there were no foot prints in the dirt. Unable to find any sign of the girl, the officer wrote it off as being an "unfounded" report. He wasn't about to tell anyone he was seeing things.

No one wants to be considered as being prone to hallucinations. Police officers avoid talking about anything that might cause people to think they were anything but rational, logical, unflappable folks who never see or do anything out of the ordinary.

During my research I spoke with several Campus Police Officers. They were all friendly especially when they found out I was retired from the Border Patrol. Several of the officers had stories to tell with the caveat I not use their names. I also spoke to a few officers no longer working for Laredo College.

This doesn't mean they never have paranormal encounters. They just never talk about them. Not until after retirement or reaching the point in their careers where they aren't worried about others opinions. The happiest days in your career are the day they pin your badge on and the day you reach twenty years and are "immune" from just about any damage you can do to your reputation.

The same little girl has been seen walking along the walkway in front of the chapel. Late at night people have seen a little girl dress in old style clothing walking along as if heading someplace. Whenever anyone tries to approach her she vanishes.

She has also been seen in front of the hospital.

The Laredo Police cruise through the college all the time. It gives extra security to the college and it gives the officers something to look at late at night.

One night, a Laredo Officer was driving slowly along the streets of the college. As he was driving, he spotted what looked like a small girl, standing on top of one of the trash cans, using the lid as a pedestal. He drove up next to her and she jumped from the trash can onto the hood of his vehicle.

This is not the kind of thing you should do if you don't want to upset a police officer. He slammed on the brakes and jumped out of his car. The girl was nowhere to be seen. She had vanished without a trace.

He described her as being about seven to eight years old and dressed in old style clothing like from the turn of the century. Not wanting to appear as someone who sees things the officer never put this down on any official report but he did mention it to some of his friends. A few of them said they'd seen the same girl walking around the college at one time or another.

On the second night of investigations Ismael and Dr. Ricardo J. Solis, the College President, were walking around the old stable area which is now the motor pool. Ismael had a thermal camera showing Dr. Solis how the device worked.

As they were walking, an image showed up in blue. On the thermal camera people give off heat and show up as white or red. Anything blue means it is cold. The blue image looked to be about the height of a young girl.

The thermal camera had been used all evening and the memory chip was full. Ismael was unable to record the blue image. It looked about the size of a young girl.

In 1870 Fort McIntosh was expanded by building a hospital, post office, and quarter master's store house. These were all wooden structures built with materials shipped in from the north east.

The officers took over the patients ward and used it as their billet. A billet is the living quarters, where a soldier is assigned to sleep. In the past, a billet was a private home ordered to accept soldiers. Soldiers were generally billeted in barracks or garrisons when not on combat duty and such accommodations were available. Any sick or injured men were sent into town to be cared for at the local hospital.

The Third Amendment to the United States Constitution places restrictions on the quartering of soldiers in private homes without the owner's consent, forbidding the practice in peacetime. The British Government had come up with the "Quartering Acts" in the late 1700s. Citizens were forced to lodge troupes whether they wanted to or not. This included feeding the men which would become an expensive undertaking. When troupes first arrived in Laredo, Texas the citizens were allowed to decide if they would house the soldiers or not. It was financially beneficial since the United States Government was paying for food and lodging.

The first hospital was replaced in 1885 with the current structure near Washington Street Bridge. At the time there were only a few buildings at Fort McIntosh. It was a two story brick structure. There was a porch running all around the ground floor. The hospital has had some weird activity as well.

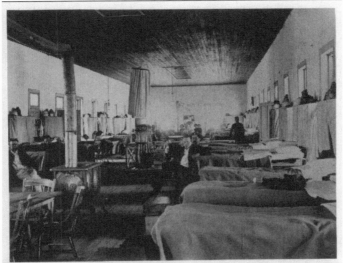

Troupes stationed at Fort McIntosh were housed in the 1870 hospital.
Photo curtesy of the National Archives.

One night while driving by, the police heard what sounded like dogs barking from the inside the building. They walked around looking in all the windows and checking the doors. How could a pack of dog have gained entry? Using the key, the officers opened the front door and walked in, carefully, in case the dogs were hostile. As soon as the door was open the barking stopped.

The ground floor was empty so they clomb the stairs. Nothing upstairs either. They checked everywhere looking for how the dogs had gotten in and where they might be hiding. They could find nothing.

Joe Rogerio is a long time Paranormal Investigator. He has been looking into the paranormal since 2008. He says he loves God and Jesus Christ without getting preachy about it. He's also a proud American. Joe was born in Laredo but raised in Corpus Christi, Texas. He travelled back and forth to visit family during the time.

He read as much about UFOs and the paranormal as he could find. His favorite books are "Skinwalkers" by Tony Hillerman and "Frankenstein" by Mary Shelley. He found his first issue of "UFO Magazine" in 1977. He loves to star gaze and this tends to lead to UFO sightings.

Joe Rogerio

When not out looking for flying saucers or ghosts, Joe is researching the legendary homeland of the Aztecs known as Aztlan. He has visited many rock art sites looking into pictographs and petroglyphs. This goes hand in hand with his outdoors enthusiasm where he can camp and fish to his heart's content. You might see Joe driving around Laredo in his 1973 Buick Electra 225.

In 2006 Joe worked as a subcontractor at Laredo Junior College which was on Fort McIntosh. His job included the maintenance of a Continues Air Monitor Station located near the old cemetery, just north of the hospital.

The unit was a small trailer which was stationed inside an eight foot high fence ringed with Concertina wire. The equipment was valuable and the gate was to be locked anytime he or his boss either entered or exited.

Late one night, as Joe was in the process of doing readings. He was nearly overwhelmed by a smell of cologne, as if someone had bathed in the stuff and was standing right beside him.

An "Olfactory Manifestation" is when you smell something related to someone from the past. Perfume is a common discovery. Pipe smoke can also be detected while looking through a possibly haunted location. Sulfur is almost always related to demons instead of ghosts.

Joe wasn't doing ghost investigations at the fort yet. He did step outside to see who might have snuck into the fenced in area around the trailer. Once outside he could still catch a whiff of cologne. There were only two keys to the gate so Joe called his boss to see if he had swung by and then left. His boss was nowhere near the station. With an uneasy feeling Joe went back to work.

Later on in the same location Joe was inside preparing some air samples when he heard the sound of the door opening. There was a spring attached to a chain that kept the door from opening too wide. The chain was rattling.

Joe turned to see if his boss was coming in. The door swung

open but there was no one there. This wasn't just some trailer door. It was heavy and had a substantial locking mechanism. Kind of like the locking device on an industrial freezer. The door continued to open until it came to the end of the chain.

Joe looked at the opening wondering if maybe his boss was trying to mess with him. Getting up and walking over, he looked out the door. The gate was still locked. No one could have gotten the gate open without making some noise.

Joe stepped outside thinking just maybe the person who opened it had walked to the other side of the trailer. The area inside the fence was empty except for him. The door had apparently opened on its own. There was no wind so why did the door swing all the way to the end of the chain?

This combined with the earlier incident got Joe to thinking maybe there was some unseen unknown force acting up in the area around the cemetery.

To try catching any anomalies, Joe began carrying his camera and voice recorder to work. When time allowed he would step outside and take a few photos.

Fort McIntosh Cemetery Entrance.

In 2008 while working with another ghost enthusiast, Cindy, the pair walked into the cemetery to see if anything could be caught on a photo. They caught a bright orb inside the stone walls. There is a monument placed in the center of the cemetery.

Fort McIntosh Cemetery Monument.

The former occupants of the cemetery were supposed to have been removed. Remains from frontier posts in Texas, Fort Ringgold, Fort Clark, and Fort McIntosh were relocated to Fort Sam Houston back in 1947 when the forts were closed. There are some rumors that say some of the bodies might have been missed either on purpose or by accident.

I have heard about construction workers unearthing a body near the East Wall. This story has been passed around by several people. I could find no record of it having happened, but stranger things have transpired and it just might be true.

Joe and Cindy walked around a bit asking questions. An EVP is made when you ask a question using a voice recorder and then wait for a possible answer. You don't hear the answer until you play the recording back and listen. Sometimes the answers are faint and hard to hear, and other times you know exactly what is being said.

After trying a few questions, Joe thought it might help if he used some military references. He asked, "Soldier, what is your rank?" Then they both waited to give the recorder a chance to catch any responses.

After a while with nothing to show for their efforts Joe and Cindy went and sat in his vehicle so they could listen to the recorder. As they sat there playing back the audio, at the moment when Joe asked for the rank, a distinct voice said, "Lieutenant...." Followed by a name which they couldn't quite make out.

This sent chills down both their spines.

Joe did a lot of solo investigations at the fort. On one night he set up his equipment on the steps of one of the old Officer's Dorms from the late 1800s. Joe asked a few questions to see if any spirits would like to, or were able to, communicate.

He said, "There are some devices with green lights on them. Could you go near them or answer some questions?" As he spoke the K-II fell forward off the step.

There was no wind and nothing interacted with the device on the video. The K-II simply fell forward. The machine was tilted back resting on a little stand attached to the back. In order for the unit to fall it would have to have been pushed, by someone or something.

In front of the Kazen Student Center Joe was standing holding his voice recorder. He was doing an EVP and on the recorder you could hear what sounded like a shot being fired. It wasn't loud but it was distinct. This was followed by what sounded like someone firing on an empty chamber, and then a second empty chamber. Lastly you could hear the sound of the cylinder being spun on a hand gun.

This episode was only heard on the recorder. Joe refers to this recording as the night he was "kind of shot at."

Why would a ghost try to shoot Joe? Maybe it had nothing to do with him and was only the residual sounds left over from some distant activity. The shooting that took place at the corrals, or the two sergeants story. Maybe the ghost was using the only means it had to try communicating.

One of the teachers there at the college was about to leave

her room for the day. It was about 5:30 PM and she stepped out the door to her office. She set her handbag down and put the key in the lock. As the key turned movement caught the teachers eye. Someone was moving about in the office she had just vacated. Looking back in through the window she saw a man in what looked like a khaki uniform walking in her office. He was tall and slim.

The U.S. Army used this style of uniform from the early 1900s up until the end of World War II.

The man in her office looked up at the teacher, as if seeing her there in the window. He then began walking towards her.

The teacher was overcome by fright. She knew no one could have gotten into her office. Not in the few seconds it took to close and lock the door. The man on the other side of the door was almost to her, so she turned and ran.

Leaving her purse setting on the floor and the keys still in the lock, she ran as fast as she could to the Campus Police Office. Once there she tried to describe what she had just seen and how it was impossible that it could have happened.

The Police Officers quickly went to her workplace intent on capturing the intruder or at least finding out what had scared her so badly.

Once at the office they unlocked the door and searched. It didn't take long since the office was not very big. The keys were still in the lock and the purse sitting on the floor. No one and no evidence of an intruder could be found.

Odalys

Odalys works at the Kasen Student Center. Over the years there have been some strange sightings and sounds experienced by folks working or hanging out at the center.

Room 235 contains many old photographs from the past. It looks a bit like a museum. While Odalys was in the room she began to feel a bit uneasy. Looking around she could see there was no one else in the room and nothing looked out of place. But the feeling lingered.

The room began to feel very hot as if someone had turned on an oven. This feeling only lasted a bit when the room began to grow cold. This sudden switch was odd. As she stood there wondering what was going on with the air in the room she felt as if some unseen person was pushing down on her, forcing her to the floor.

The door swung shut which was the last thing she needed. Odalys sprang to her feet and ran from the room. Once outside everything was back to normal.

This was just one experience Odalys had while working at the Kasen Center. Just before Thanks Giving, she was working in the office all alone. There is a hall that runs right behind her desk that leads from the breakroom to all the offices.

She heard the sound of one of the doors swinging open behind her. She looked up to see who was there only to see an empty doorway. As she sat there she heard something falling to the floor in one of the offices. Going to see what it was she saw the lights were on in the office. These lights are controlled by a sensor which turns the light on as you enter. The light was on as if someone were in the room but it was empty. No one could have gotten in without her seeing them.

Sitting back down at her desk, Odalys was facing a set of windows and a glass door. She saw someone walk along the hall right behind her in the reflection off the glass. Turning once more to see who was there she saw only an empty hallway.

She had heard the stories from others about seeing and hearing thing but to actually experience something was a bit unnerving.

In October Odalys took one of the tours being offered by the LPRS. She was at the Chapel when one of the students was scratched by some unseen hand.

Daniel De La Rosa

Daniel De La Rosa works at the Kasen Center as well. He retired from working for the county and went to work at the center to get out of the house and do something.

One night in August or September, he and a co-worker were cleaning the offices. The same area where Odalys had her experience. They were about to enter one of the offices when they both heard what sounded like a dog growling from under one of the tables.

Not wishing to have a run in with some dog, they stopped outside the door and tried to look under the table to see what was making the noise. There was nothing under there that might have made such a sound. The growling had gone on for enough time for them to look throughout the entire room for its cause. Not only was there no dog, there was nothing that could have made the sound.

Daniel was about to pass through the door when the growl began once more. He decided the room didn't need cleaning that badly. His partner was able to enter without any challenge. It was as if the growling was just for him.

While sitting in the breakroom at the far end of the hall, Daniel saw the reflection of a man walking through the room behind him. The man in the reflection was wearing a yellow shirt and khaki pants. Turning to see who was there in the room with him, Danial saw there was no one else around.

At the far end of the second floor walkway is the men's bathroom. Daniel went in to check on whether the room needed attention. As he reached the last stall the sound of the hand drier came on. The drier was activated by a sensor mounted just beneath the nozzle. The room was empty. There was no way anyone could have activated the drier and reached the door without being seen.

Others have told about hearing the hand drier go on and off. The LPRS did try to investigate the bathroom but nothing was found.

Sylvia Montemayor

Sylvia Montemayor told me she is not, nor has she ever been psychic. She does get feeling on occasion but considers these just intuition. Back in the 1990s Silvia was taking art classes at Laredo Junior College which became Laredo College.

Her and a group of friends decided to take a drive around the campus just to have a look around and enjoy the afternoon. It was around 4:00 PM. They took the road around the inside of the stone wall that is the perimeter of the fort. As they were approaching the old tennis courts, which used to be right across the street from the Guardhouse, a dog appeared out of nowhere. One minute there was nothing there and then the dog appeared as if from nowhere. It began chasing their car, barking and growling at them. Sylvia gave it the gas to get away from this beast. She had a distinct feeling this wasn't any normal dog.

Back in 1988 when I first arrived in Laredo, I began hearing

120

stories, reports of weird activity taking place, near the tennis courts at the college. Many people said there were Satanists performing rituals in the area. The odd thing is, a friend of mine who was also in the Border Patrol said he had driven up on a group of people performing some kind of, what to him, looked like devil worship. This had been in an area just south of the tennis courts.

Sylvia had heard these stories as well and thought maybe the dog had been some form of familiar or entity placed there to keep people away.

Later on in her studies Sylvia was taking art classes in one of the original old builds along Lamar Road. These were single story, wood frame structures, stucco over brick, and painted yellow, built back in the 1940s. Some of these buildings had basements. There were a lot of students all working in the same classroom. As they were finishing up, it was time to clean up before going home. The sinks were all being used so Sylvia and one of her friends decide to go across the hallway and use the sinks in another part of the building. They left the classroom and were moving along the dark hallway when they spotted a shape, or actually just a shadow, at the end of the hall. The shadow just kind of stayed in one place but did drift up and down just enough to see it was really there.

Sylvia had one of her feeling as if this was a ghost standing in the dark, watching them. They decided it would be better to go back and wait for the sink in the classroom.

On October 19, Sylvia showed up at the Guardhouse to take part in the tours. She was issued an Ovilus, an electronic device used to allow spirits to communicate with the living. She caught quite a bit of activity as she moved about the guardhouse.

Almost as soon as Sylvia started using the device she started getting messages. They had started investigating one of the cells at the north side of the guardhouse. She immediately started getting words such as: "thermal," "eat," "run," "general," which was interesting since they were in a fort. Sylvia also heard names like: "Veronica," "Pat," and "Jim." Two very interesting messages were the following. She got the message, "Metal." Sylvia asked if the spirit was talking about the metal bunk that was next to her. The response she got was, "Uh huh."

Sylvia also got the words, "teacher," and "English" which she thought was a reference to her job. She later learned that one of the spirits that is often captured by EVP is that of an English Teacher who said she is guarding a group of children.

Texas Mexican Railroad Caboose which sits next to the Guardhouse.

Another event which was very interesting occurred to her niece, Ariel. A group of investigators went into the Tex-Mex caboose, which sits right next to the guard house. They began to have a conversation with the spirit if Jim. Jim said, "wave," so Ariel waved one hand. She then said, "I'm sorry Jim, I'm very shy and I can't do more because I'm not alone." Jim replied, "Kiss." Jim got flirty with Sylvia's niece.

9 BETWEEN THE WARS

At the end of "The War to End All Wars" as it was known, folks got back to living their lives intent on the idea there would never be anything like what they had just gone through. Fort McIntosh was mostly idling during the years between 1918 and 1942.

Mexico was still embroiled in a revolution of their own. In 1913 President Madero had been assassinated and Victoriano Huerta declared himself the new president of Mexico. President Woodrow Wilson refused to acknowledge Huerta as being a legitimate leader. This led to tensions all along the border.

Fighting broke out in 1914 between the Constitutionalists armies of Venustiano Carranza and the Conventionalists armies of Poncho Villa and Emiliano Zapata. Huerta resigned and went into exile in July 1914. The Conventionalists won after the assassination of Zapata in 1919 and the surrender of Villa in July 1920.

The fighting on the other side of the Rio Grande kept the soldiers stationed at Fort McIntosh on their toes. The river was patrolled on a regular bases looking for bandits or military units trying to enter the United States. As many as three hundred Mexican Nationals were being held at Fort McIntosh as prisoners but not POWs. Since the United States was not at war with Mexico, any military incursions were treated as being banditry. Even when the bandits were wearing uniforms from the Mexican Army.

Troupes would be assigned to patrol the river in either direction from Laredo. They would pack their equipment which was then attached to a pack mull or horse. Once they had traveled to their assigned patrol area the troupes would establish an out post and scout the area. The patrol would ride out and follow the river looking for any signs of large groups of people coming from Mexico.

If tracks were found they would follow until the suspects were located. If nothing was found the soldiers would return to their new home away from home for anywhere from two weeks to several months at a time.

Sullivan Springs was one location soldiers used on a regular bases. There was a fresh water spring they could use and a cave that gave them shelter from the sun and rain. The soldiers would carve their names into the rock wall as a sign they had been there.

Joseph B Cravens visited this site on June 5, 1911.
He was from Rome, Texas.
Hundreds of names from the past lay buried under the collapsed cave.

Back in 1990 I visited the cave while on patrol and saw hundreds of names carved into the rock wall. Some were from 1909 all the way up to 1930s. In 2014 I revisited the cave only to find it had collapsed. Few of the carvings have survived the years. Sullivan Springs is on private property and not open to the public.

The army weren't the only ones using the spring as a camp site. Indians had used the location for years. There were pictographs on some of the rocks around the spring.

Indian Pictographs from hundreds of years ago.
Rain and wind is slowly erasing these pictures from the rocks.

The three barracks built in 1919 as troupe housing.
Photograph curtesy of Laredo Public Library.

Meanwhile on the fort, new construction was going ahead. Three brick buildings were being constructed as barracks so the men wouldn't have to live in tents any longer. The three buildings were in a row facing north. Each was two stories tall with room in the attic for storage and a basement for heating and storage. Only Arechiga Hall remains standing today.

Training is a constant in the military. Guarding, training and cleaning is the day to day norm. Having just fought in a worldwide conflict, soldiers were keeping up with the latest weapons. The hand grenade has been around for hundreds of years. The major drawback was the grenade could only be thrown as far as the soldier was physically able.

During World War I a grenade was developed that could be launched from the end of a rifle barrel. The bullet would impact the base of the grenade and the grenade could then be fired up to 200 yards.

Men at Fort McIntosh used rifle grenades while in training.

On occasion things got dropped or lost while moving about on the training maneuvers.

On March 23, 1919, two young boys were playing in the field on Goodwin Farm, next to Fort McIntosh. Pedro Trevino picked up a round metal object laying in the dirt. As his younger brother moved away, he accidently activated the object.

The blast was powerful enough to kill anyone within a 75 yard radius. The younger brother was just outside the blast zone. Pedro was killed instantly.

Having just come out of a major conflict and people being hesitant to appear unpatriotic, no charges were ever leveled and no investigation into where the grenade came from ever persuade.

Pedro's death was written off as an unfortunate accident.

In 1919, the men at Fort McIntosh proposed creating a Baseball League. This would consist of four teams. One made up from the 37th Infantry. One from the Knights of Columbus. A team would come from Nuevo Laredo, and one from Laredo. The ball players met at the City Fire Hall to hammer out the details.

Since Fort McIntosh had a ball diamond the games would be played there. Citizens wishing to watch would be welcomed to the fort.

The first swimming pool was built at Fort McIntosh as well. It was for use of the enlisted men so they could cool off after a long day of army life. The pool was put in just north of two warehouses near the south gate. This is where the Allied Health Buildings are today. People have asked why the Allied Health

Buildings look so odd. When the old warehouses were torn down, the historic society insisted the new buildings look like the originals.

In August, 1919 there were some reports of a ghost hanging out at a boarding house and saloon near Fort McIntosh. The boarding house was a part of the I&GN rail station. The International Great Northern Railroad, or I&GN, operated in Texas. It was created on September 30, 1873, when International Railroad and the Houston and Great Northern Railroad merged. Texas and Mexico Railway, bought the I&GN in June 30, 1924.

People would report seeing a man, dressed in a soldier's uniform sitting on a beer barrel. He was holding a bottle in one hand and looked to be asleep or passed out. When anyone tried to wake him the soldier would fade away into nothing.

The soldier was seen by several people all of whom thought he was real up until he disappeared. On a few occasions footsteps could be herd coming down the stairs from the second floor. When someone would look up the stairs to see who was coming down, the stairs would be empty.

On September 13, 1919, troupes of Company I, 37th Infantry where ordered to Corpus Christi to the Rest Camp for a much needed time away from the fort. Captain Egeland marched his men to the Railroad Station and they boarded the east bound train. The captain's wife was allowed to accompany her husband.

The trip east was mostly uneventful but as they were nearing Corpus Christi it began to rain, hard. Weather is something you put up with in the army so the men assembled at the station and marched to the camp which was just north of the city.

The rain storm turned into a hurricane. The residents of Corpus Christi weren't concerned. They had weathered a storm just three years earlier and the Barrier Islands had done their job then and they should do their job this time as well.

The hurricane made landfall twenty-five miles south from the city. The north-east side of a hurricane is the most dangerous place in a storm. This put Corpus Christi and the men at the Rest Camp in a bad place. The storm surge was sixteen feet. This flooded most low lying areas and the camp was washed away along with the men of the 37th Infantry.

Coastal city Corpus Christi was hit by a devastating hurricane on September 14, 1919. Names weren't given to hurricanes until the 1940s. The city was torn to pieces and in need of help. Between two and six hundred people died in the 1919 hurricane. A sixteen foot storm surge inundated the low-lying areas of Corpus Christi, destroying almost all of the wooden buildings there. Port Aransas was nearly totally demolished.

When word reached Laredo, and then Fort McIntosh, everyone got busy putting together a relief effort. The medical staff at the fort hospital put together packages of drugs and bandages. Stretchers and surgical equipment all went into boxes and crates. Everything was sent to the rail station for transport. The medical staff were detailed to Corpus for the duration of the emergency, along with Captain Hakler and Company K, of the 37th Infantry.

Citizens in Laredo took clothing and food to the fort to be shipped to the city 150 miles to their east. Volunteers assembled and were sent along with the provisions to help look for survivors and take care of the wounded.

As searchers began to comb the area looking for survivors they came across a body in military uniform. When they looked closer they discovered it was the body of a young woman. At the time women's uniforms were far different from the men's uniforms. The searchers wondered why this woman was dressed

130

like a man.

Tour boat known as the Japonica beached by the 1919 Storm
Photograph compliments of L. H. Gross Collection
Texas A&M University, Corpus Christi, Texas

It turned out this was Mrs. Egeland, the wife of Captain Egeland. She is believed to have put on one of her husband's uniforms, to make moving through the storm water less burdensome than trying it in a dress.

She had drown at one point in her escape attempt and her body washed ashore the next day. Later on her husband's body was found as well.

Of the twenty-two men of Company I, 37th Infantry none of their bodies were found or identified.

People clearing the rubble caused by the storm around the
Corpus Christi Railway and Light Company
Photograph compliments of L. H. Gross Collection
Texas A&M University, Corpus Christi, Texas

The train coming from Fort McIntosh made it as far as Alice before they found the tracks were under water. The storm surge had pushed water fifty miles inland from the coast.

The conductor didn't like the idea of traveling through the water because there was no way of knowing if the rails were still in place or if they had been washed away. With the mission in mind it was decided to proceed at a much reduced pace. They had to keep an eye on the tracks ahead of them as they moved, stopping to remove large debris as they went. The train arrived outside Corpus Christ after midnight of the 16th. There was no way to travel any farther since buildings had been pushed onto the tracks and the station had been destroyed. When Captain Hakler was told about the bodies of Captain and Mrs. Egeland he sent word back to Laredo.

Bodies began piling up in any buildings still intact enough to not be a hazard. A school was used to house some of the dead but soon it became necessary to remove any dead and bury them. None of the men of Company I, 37th Infantry were ever identified.

Soldiers from Company K, 37th Infantry, were instrumental in rescuing 12 people stranded on the second floor of the hotel.

After weeks of unpleasant work, the men were returned to Fort McIntosh.

Anytime a large group of people are living in one location for a long time there is certain activity that has to be taken care of. At Fort McIntosh the use of outhouses continued up until 1919. That year, the fort was treated to an improvement involving the use of trenching machines to dig in a system of sewer pipes. This was considered such an occasion the citizens of Laredo were invited to the fort to watch the construction in progress. People made the trip out to watch this new development.

For months a company dug trenches and then installed clay pipes to haul away the sewage. This was considered quite a modern development.

Juan Flores was working, laying sewer pipe in the bottom of the trenches. He was in the bottom of an eight foot deep trench when the sides collapsed, burying him under nearly a ton of dirt.

His fellow workers ran to his rescue only to become trapped up to their hips in falling dirt. More men had to come help dig out the would be rescuers. This led to an hour delay before Juan could be pulled from the bottom of the trench. His body was taken to his home so his family could arrange for burial.

In Germany, the Quartiermeister, or master of quarters, was the senior soldier responsible for lodgings and provisions. Since the time of Baron von Steuben, the United States Army has used German terminology. In the United States Army the Quarter Master is responsible for supplies.

With hundreds of men all together in one place you're bound to get some bad apples. One of these was Walter Nicholson. Late one night in 1925, he broke into the Quarter Masters warehouse and tried to make off with supplies. He was arrested, convicted, and sentenced to ten years at Leavenworth Military Prison.

Benjamin Gregory assaulted a guard by hitting him in the head with a hammer and then escaping from the fort. He was arrested, convicted, and sentenced to two years in Leavenworth.

As these men were waiting for transportation to their new home for the next few years, they somehow managed to convince the guard on duty, Private Archuleta, to allow them to escape. At 2:00 A.M. one September night, the guard opened the cells and allowed six prisoners to slip away and then went with them as they left the fort.

The seven fugitives headed north trying to disappear into the interior. They were travelling across the Callaghan Ranch when they were spotted by Patrol Inspector H.C. Ramsey. Ramsey drew his pistol and went to arrested the band of escapees.

Gregory managed to slip away into the brush before Ramsey knew how many men he was dealing with. A ranch hand was deputized to assist in transporting the soldiers back to Fort McIntosh. Once the prisoners were back at the fort, the guards discovered Gregory was still missing.

Benjamin Gregory decided he was better off in Mexico so he made his way back south intent on crossing into Nuevo Laredo. He crossed the bridge and began his long walk to Monterrey where he hoped to disappear.

The commander of Fort McIntosh had sent word to the Immigration Officials to be on the lookout for Gregory, but he had managed to slip by them without being discovered. Thinking he was home free, he took off heading south.

The U.S. Immigration Officials had passed on the disruption of the missing soldier to their counter parts in Nuevo Laredo. Wishing to reestablish good relations with the United States, Mexico City had encouraged government officials to cooperate as much as possible.

A patrol working twenty miles south of town, encountered a man walking along the road who matched the description of the missing prisoner. The Mexican Immigration took the man into custody and transported him back to Nuevo Laredo.

Once in town the Mexican Officials contacted the U.S. Immigration and turned the man over to them. Benjamin Gregory was taken back to Fort McIntosh where he now faced charges of desertion, and illegal escape. This added many years to the two he had tried to avoid.

A lot of soldiers don't know this and are surprised when they find out. If a soldier has one year left on his, or her, enlistment and he winds up being arrested and spending time in the guard house or prison, his enlistment is placed on hold until he is released back to the army. He then has to fulfil his enlistment because the time spent in custody doesn't count towards his military time. If he is convicted of a serious crime he will face receiving a Dishonorable Discharge.

A military fort is very much like a small city. They have housing, dining facilities, a post exchange which is a store, and some will have a fire department. Fort McIntosh had a fire brigade made up of soldiers from several different companies.

On November 17, 1926 smoke was seen coming from a store at the intersection of Convent and Hidalgo. The people working at the Valdes Building called for the Laredo Fire Department and then got busy trying to save any valuables they could.

As the Laredo Fire Department was arriving on scene, the soldiers at Fort McIntosh saw the smoke billowing into the sky. Knowing there was trouble in the down town area the fire brigade assembled and then drove their fire truck to the scene of the fire. The two fire crews worked hand in hand getting a crew to the second floor where the blaze was located. They managed to put the fire out after thirty minutes of hard work. The store on the first floor suffered water damage and the employees of the Franklin Brothers had to remove all the wet merchandize.

The Laredo Fire Department and the Fort McIntosh Fire Brigade worked together on several situations throughout their history.

At the beginning of 1928, there were over five hundred soldiers stationed at the fort. The buildings were overcrowded. The decision was made to transfer the 4th Field Artillery to Fort Robinson in Nebraska. The 3rd Field Artillery was to be sent to Camp Knox in Kentucky. This left only fifteen men at the fort.

The 8th Combat Engineers were to move into the now mostly vacant military base. This would change the focus of training from canon fire to construction and destruction. If it needed to be built during battle or it was to be blown up, Combat Engineers were involved.

On September 30, 1929 a body was found floating in the

river near Laredo. It was taken to the coroner's office and determined to have died from drowning but there was no means of identifying him. The body was buried at the City Cemetery as "Unknown." This happened more often than people could imagen.

A week later, during roll call, Corporal Edgar Cooper, from Muskogee, Oklahoma was found missing and unaccounted for. When the Army Officials contacted Laredo to see if they had any unknown personal in their jail, they were told of the body found Monday of the previous week.

The body was exhumed and then identified as being the missing soldier, 27 year old Corporal Cooper with seven years of army service.

An investigation lead to discovering the Corporal had been seen on Friday, the 27th as he left the front gate. The investigators believed he may have tried to swim the river and drowned but there was nothing to support this theory. There were no signs of any foul play. He was reburied at the fort cemetery.

In the army, you go where the army wants you. Men who joined in Laredo, sometimes wound up scattered all over the country. Enrique Arechiga was born in Nuevo Laredo and joined the 4th Artillery Battalion in U.S. Army in 1926. He became an artillery man and after a year, he was transferred to Fort Crocket in Galveston. There he became a part of the Coastal Artillery Battalion.

Sometime in mid-1930 he noticed a swollen place on his neck but didn't think it was that bad. He chose to ignore it. What he had found was called a carbuncle, an infected hair follicle. The infection grew to a point it infected his blood system and led to septicemia.

Enrique died on November 6, 1930. His body was shipped back to Fort McIntosh and he was buried in the fort cemetery.

The fort wasn't all military activity. At one time the men at Fort McIntosh had their own polo club. When the people from Laredo came out to watch, they soon decided to create their own polo team which then competed with the men at the fort.

Boxing was an all-time favorite. Swede Berg was a soldier and boxer. He would practice any time he had time away from guard duty, or K.P. or training. In July, Swede Berg had a match with The White Wolf from Nuevo Laredo.

On the weekends Swede would take a stroll across the bridge to see the sights and maybe enjoy a drink. November 28th, 1927 was one of his days away from the fort. He'd spent the day in Nuevo Laredo and was on his way back to the bridge when a man approached him and said he was a police officer. Swede needed to follow this man to the station.

Not knowing if he had done something wrong or there was some minor complaint, Swede began following the man. Up until he noticed the man was not walking towards the police station.

Swede hesitated thinking he should make a run for it when the man pulled a gun and order him into an alleyway. Instead of obeying Swede sent an uppercut right to the man's jaw. The would be robber crumpled to the ground unconscious.

Being a law abiding citizen, Swede stood there waiting for the real police to come. When they arrived the assailant was regaining consciousness. Swede gave his story to the real officer who didn't understand him.

The assailant began saying Swede had attacked him for no reason. Only hearing one side of the situation even with two witnesses saying Berg was not the perpetrator, the officer took Swede into custody.

When the commanding officer heard about the arrest he contacted the US Consulate in Nuevo Laredo and asked him to look into the situation. The Consulate visited Swede in jail and relayed his side of the story to the police. It took a few days to get the charges dropped and Swede released.

Swede continued his boxing but his visits to Mexico were at an end.

There were wrestling bouts held at the fort. In 1930 Gus Kallio fought Tsutoa Hegami from Japan. They brought in boxers like Gentleman Jim Corbett in February, 1933. The boxing, and wrestling matches were held at the fort gymnasium and open to the public.

The men at the fort would sponsor a picnic. Music would be performed by the fort band and people would bring food and lounge about the open parade grounds.

Each year Texas A&M began sending Cadets to Fort McIntosh for extended training. Students taking Engineering classes would be sent to Laredo to receive advanced training by the soldiers stationed there. This training would last about six weeks.

Prohibition had been enacted in January, 1920. It made the manufacture, transportation, and sale of alcohol illegal. The 18th amendment to the constitution did nothing to stop crime. Instead it lead to a whole new form of organized crime.

Alcohol was still legal in both Mexico and Canada so people

began importing their own even though this could land them in trouble.

A new shape of bottle came on the market. It was thin and slightly curved. The name given was "Hip Flask" but no one ever carried them in their hip pockets.

Folks would walk into Mexico and purchase a bottle or two of alcohol. They would shove the bottles into their boots, place their pants legs over the boots, and then walk back into the United States. This is where the term, "Boot Legging" comes from.

As more and more people wanted to buy alcohol the price and therefor the profits went up. This led to smuggling going into overdrive. People began sneaking larger and larger quantities of illegal drinks into the country.

In November, 1931, five smugglers stepped out on a landing in Mexico just south of the Indian Crossing. They surveyed the river looking for any sign of the police or Border Patrol. Once they were convinced the coast was clear, one man slipped into the water to swim into the United States pulling a huge bag filled with bottles of alcohol, while the others kept an eye out for anyone on the U.S. side.

What the smugglers didn't realize was, there were four Border Patrol Agents waiting in the brush on Fort McIntosh side of the river.

As the smuggler began to pull himself up onto the bank near the North Wall the agents came out of hiding. They had spotted the man in mid-river but were not aware of the four still in Mexico.

As the agents tried to arrest the smuggler, the men in Mexico began shooting at them. The smuggler may have been hit by one of his own men because he was shot in the shoulder and leg as he tried to dive back into the river.

The agents dove for cover and returned fire.

Bullets went back and forth between the two sides for a few minutes before the men in Mexico decided it was time to run. They grabbed the smuggler and drug him away with them. He was treated at the local hospital and then released. As far as the Mexican Officials were concerned, nothing illegal had taken place.

The agents were unhurt but shook up by the incident. The bag full of alcohol was swept away down river.

Horses were used by the army from the very first day of its creation. Not just cavalry but for mounted infantry and to haul all manner of equipment. With new ideas comes inventions. Even during World War I horses were used to transport men and equipment.

In 1934, Fort McIntosh began to phase out beasts of burden and replace them with motorized vehicles. The stables were closed and all four legged occupants shipped out to other military locations. By June the fort had become totally mechanized. There were several motor pools where vehicles could be parked and maintained. Infantry would ride into battle in the backs of trucks or on motorcycles. Even though the army had been using motorcycles since 1915 horses had still been the main form of transport.

Horses had their maintenance problems. They had to be fed so huge buildings had to be erected to store food. Rats would run through the hay and their droppings would lead to sickness. Every fort had to have their own veterinarian unit. Troupes had to be trained on how to treat sick and injured animals.

And horses created manure that had to be dealt with.

With the transition to an all mechanized fort, new issues arose. Gasoline had to be stored on the fort. This could be a fire hazard so precautions had to be in place. Mechanics had to be trained and housed on the fort. Parts had to be kept on hand to replace things as they broke or wore out from driving over roads that were less that animal trails.

It's hard to imagen there had been air planes at Fort McIntosh since 1911, but it took twenty-three years before trucks were being used instead of horses.

On July 14, 1935, in Nuevo Laredo, Santiago Esparza killed his wife Rosala. He then ran for the border, swimming the river into the United States.

The police found Rosala's body and began looking for her husband. After searching the neighborhood they were told Santiago was last seen entering the river. Chief Rodriguez contacted his counterpart in Laredo requesting assistance in looking for the murder suspect.

Assistant Chief Rafael Villarreal was met at the bridge by Laredo Police and escorted to Fort McIntosh which was right across the river from the scene of the crime.

Soldiers at the fort assisted in searching all along the river. The searchers worked for hours moving from the river inland and searching the fields on both sides of the installation. After spending the entire day looking, Esparza was never found.

The warrant for the arrest of Santiago Esparza was never served. There was a real possibility the witnesses who told the Nuevo Laredo Police Esparza had fled into the United States were mistaken or gave falls information to assist in his escape.

Jesus Wise was born in Laredo sometime around the end of the 1800s. Some of the records from back then are missing. He went to the Laredo schools and graduated from Laredo High School around 1910.

In 1921, Jesus was chosen for jury duty to decide the fate of a man accused of murder. Santiago Armenta was accused of murdering Vicente Vega on September 4, 1920. Santiago was found guilty and sentenced to death. Jesus would have had to cast a guilty decision for the case to have a capital punishment verdict.

As a young adult Jesus was interested in baseball so he joined the "Milmo" baseball team. They would play against other teams in Webb County usually winding up at the Fort McIntosh Ball Diamond. Jesus became the manager shortly after joining.

In 1926 he moved to the "Oilers," another Laredo team that would practice and compete at the fort.

Jesus was married and had several children. He got into politics and was the Webb County Delegate to the Democrat Convention in 1930. He then joined the Webb County Tax Office as the Chief Deputy Tax Assessor. By 1934, Jesus had moved to Austin to work at the State Comptroller's Office. During the course of his duties Jesus was sent back to Laredo. There he met Ethel Carlos.

Ethel was 19 and worked at her parent's restaurant in downtown Laredo. She lived with her parents at 2304 Victoria, right across the tracks from the fort. Ethel became pregnant.

The couple moved to San Antonio and presented themselves as being married. Once the baby was born Ethel moved back home to Laredo and moved back in with her parents. Jesus followed her and began visiting her and the baby on occasion.

On August 11, 1935, Ethel and her parents had been out for a drive. As they pulled into their driveway Jesus pulled in right behind them. He said he wanted to speak with Ethel. Ethel's folks went inside as the two began to talk at the curb.

Private Jones lived right across the street from the Carlos. He was married to one of Ethel's sisters. When Jesus had driven up Jones was standing on his porch and watched as the two began to talk. When it looked as if it would be just a casual conversation, Jones went inside. A scream from across the street brought him outside in a rush. He saw Ethel stumbling from Jesus' car and trying to get to her home. The baby was clutched in her arms but fell as she was trying to open the gate. Ethel landed on the ground halfway inside the gate.

Jesus jumped from his car and ran after her. He then stood over her saying, "If I can't have you. I'd rather kill you." He then stabbed himself in the neck with a knife he'd been holding. Jesus feel to the ground next to Ethel.

Jones ran across the street to help his sister-in-law. He saw there was blood all over the front of her dress. Some was from Jesus but most was coming from a gash in her throat. Scooping Ethel up in his arms, Jones ran back across the street to his car. He jumped in and drove quickly onto the fort.

Jones' wife had run outside along with her husband. She grabbed the baby and tried to comfort it. As she stood there clutching the infant, Jesus got back to his feet. Blood was all down the front of his shirt but he didn't seem to care. He walked back to his car. Got in. And drove away.

Private William Guthrie had been on guard duty at the Victoria Street Entrance to the fort. He waved Jones through knowing the other private was heading to the base hospital which was just a block away. Private Guthrie had witnessed the attack but was unable to interfere from where he was stationed.

Doctor Joshua Cocke was on duty at the hospital as Private Jones came running in with Ethel in his arms. He had Jones place Ethel on the operating table and went to work trying to save the young woman's life. He did his best but Ethel had lost too much blood and she died after a few minutes.

Jesus Wise turned himself into the Laredo Police Department later that night. He was placed in a cell to await his trial for murder.

While waiting in his cell, Jesus began to grow ill. He was diagnosed as having kidney disease and needed an operation to save his life. He was transferred to San Antonio, but the question was, who was going to pay for the operation? His crime had taken place in Laredo but he was now housed in San Antonio. Even without the operation Jesus recovered in time for his trial.

Due to the publicity in the case, the trial was moved to Carrizo Springs.

During the trail the jury heard that Jesus Wise was already married and had children as old as Ethel. The prosecution dug out any and all dirt they could find.

Jesus tried to claim Ethel had stabbed him in the neck before she ran away and then stabbed herself. Privates Guthrie, and Jones didn't see Jesus stab Ethel but they did see Jesus stab himself while standing over her body. Jesus Wise was found guilty of second degree murder and sentenced to twenty-five years in prison.

There is no record of his ever leaving prison alive. Ethel was buried at the Laredo City Cemetery.

In 1936 a group of thirty Boy Scouts were enroute to Corpus Christy for a summer program. The bus arrived in Laredo and stopped for gas while the Scout Master asked where the town's camp was. The gas station attendant wasn't sure where to send them so he suggested the scouts head over to the fort, saying maybe they could help.

The bus took the scouts over to the fort to ask about quarters for the night.

The soldiers at Fort McIntosh were more than glad to put the boys up for the night and allowed them to use the chow hall, and sleep in the barracks. For a bunch of boys in the 1930s this was probably quite a treat.

In the morning D.P. Barrow, the District Boy Scout Commissioner tried to pass on word that Laredo had a Boy Scout Camp that could accommodate one hundred boys. He told people in Laredo, from then on, they should contact any one of the Boy Scout Officials and they would direct them to the Camp Richter.

In 1940 the idea came up once more of moving Fort McIntosh to a new location. The fort and soldiers would be located on the North East side of town and the present location would be turned into a Tuberculosis Hospital.

Tuberculosis has been around for thousands of years. Mummified remains from ancient Egypt have been found with tuberculosis markers. This disease has been responsible for the deaths of more people than all other diseases combined. TB was believed to be caused by vampires at one time. In the 1800s TB was called Consumption because it looked as if the victim was slowly being consumed from the inside.

Albert Calmette and Camille Guérin developed the first genuinely successful immunization against tuberculosis in 1906, using attenuated bovine-strain tuberculosis. It was called bacille Calmette–Guérin (BCG). The BCG vaccine was first used on humans in 1921 in France, but achieved widespread acceptance in the US, Great Britain, and Germany only after World War II.

The best recourse for most patients in the United States was to isolate them in hospitals or sanitariums. The only treatment was surgical intervention, including the "Pneumothorax Technique," that required collapsing the infected lung so it could "rest" and allow tuberculous lesions to heal. In 1946 the development of the antibiotic Streptomycin made effective treatment and a cure for TB a reality.

After examining the possibility of moving the fort and turning the property into a hospital was finally considered unmanageable and never came about.

In 1940, airplanes wishing to land in Laredo only had one place they could use. Fort McIntosh Air Field. The field was on the north end of the fort and could handle most small planes of the time.

Air travel was becoming more innovative and the people living in Laredo wanted to see about having their own air field installed. A delegation went to Washington to see if funds could be obtained to build a modern air field. County Judge M. Raymond was in Washington while Judge John Valls took care of things in Laredo. The field was to be named "Colonel John H. Zachery Air Field." Colonel Zachery had been at Fort McIntosh for many years and was instrumental in creating and enhancing aviation while at the fort.

Judge Raymond was able to get funding through the Works Progress Administration to pay for the construction of an air field to the east of town. Once construction had begun, the

WPA transferred the construction to the National Defense Project.

In January, 1941, at 10:45 A.M. a small airplane flew over the air field. It looked as if the pilots was looking over the construction of the site. The plane flew north and then began to bank to the right. Suddenly the aircraft went into a spiral and crashed to the ground at the Number 4 Green at the Country Club. The grounds keeper was working nearby and watched as the plane impacted the ground and burst into flames.

The pilot, Captain Eugene Tips was thrown from the plane and landed hard enough to fracture his neck, back and pelvis. He died soon after the crash. Technical Sergeant Hector Chessi was killed inside the plane.

Soldiers from the fort were rushed to the crash site to recover the bodies and retrieve the plane. There was nothing to explain why the plane crashed. The bodies were sent to a funeral home in Laredo until arrangements could be made to send them back to their home towns.

Once the air field was completed, Webb County bought the land from the owners and then leased it to the government for a dollar a year. Total cost in building the air field was $45,000 and it covered 1,500 acres. A rail line was built to connect Fort McIntosh to the air field for transportation of materials from one site to the other.

In the spring of 1941, General Pyron was notified of a training exercise being held at Fort Bliss in El Paso, Texas. The training would last for several weeks and he and his men were ordered to participate. There was little threat requiring the army's attention so the soldiers packed their gear and moved to the railroad station.

Ninety men were left at the fort. Mostly administration, medical personal and men not required to participate in the training.

On May 30, 1941 a report arrived at Fort McIntosh saying saboteurs were going to blow up the international bridge crossing from Laredo to Nuevo Laredo as well as the railroad bridge. There was a list of thirty men living in town who were believed to be anarchists, and they were supposed to be "heavily armed."

The colonel in charge scrambled to find personnel to guard the bridges. Once all the personnel at the fort had been accounted for, there were not enough men available to guard both the fort and the bridge. To make matters worse, most of the weapons had gone with the soldiers travelling to El Paso.

Civilians from Laredo were called on to form a home guard. These men combined with the few soldiers and Laredo Police Officers moved to the bridges and spent the next few weeks watching for an attack from anarchists or communists.

To see to it the Home Guard received training, they spent time at the fort learning how to use a 45 caliber pistol and a few needed extra instructions.

Once it was determined the attack on the bridge was unfounded, the home guard were released and the soldiers returned to the fort. General Pyron and the well trained soldiers arrived a week after the crisis had expired.

10 WORLD WAR II

Many people in Laredo consider the sandstone wall running around Laredo College to be the defining boundary of the old fort. The wall looks ancient and a fort should have a wall around it.

During the Great Depression, FDR created a jobs program to put people back to work. The idea being, it was better to earn a living and feel good about yourself than to simply receive a handout.

In 1939 the Work Projects Administration created jobs to improve the country while giving people work to do. Roads and bridges were built all over the country. In Texas the Civilian Conservation Corps was responsible for just about every building put up on State Park lands.

Local citizens acquired land and enlisted the Civilian Conservation Corps to build a park. After construction was completed, the park was donated to the state. The park opened June 1, 1941, and was named for John Nance "Cactus Jack" Garner. Garner was a Uvalde native who served as vice president of the United States from 1933 to 1941, the first two terms of President Roosevelt's time in office.

The original Park Entrance going into Garner State Park.
The stonework was done by the CCC.
Lourdes James standing just inside the park.

Japan attacked Pearl Harbor on the morning of Dec. 7, 1941, and the United States went to war once again.

Laredo had a need for the WPA so construction was begun on a wall that enclosed Fort McIntosh. Stone masons were brought in and sand stone was quarried and shipped to Laredo. Laborers were hired to help clear land and haul stone. About ninety locals were employed on the project. The wall was finished in 1942. Up until that time the boundaries of the fort were mostly just a line in the dirt. The wall was finished shortly after Japan had attacked Pearl Harbor bringing the United States into the Second World War.

Sandstone Wall around Fort McIntosh.
The brick column was added much later than the original wall.

The year the wall was finished, and eleven months after the attack at Pearl Harbor, the army was preparing the country for war. London was being bombed by the Luftwaffe. The Civil Defense was tasked with the mission of blacking out the city at night so the Germans couldn't see their targets. Thinking there was a possibility of bombers attacking the United States, perhaps flying north out of Mexico, Laredo began practice air raid drills.

Mayor Cluck, the Command Staff of Fort McIntosh, and the head of the Civil Defense Commander Al Notzon, were all told of the upcoming drill but no one beyond these few people knew it was coming.

This marker is at the base of one of the buildings used by the Army Reserve Unit at Laredo College.

Officials took up their positions atop the Hamilton Hotel and watched the city just moments before the siren went off. As the air raid siren blared the men atop the hotel watches as lights quickly went out.

Cars driving along the streets would stop and the drivers would turn off their lights. The city did a good job extinguishing any sources of illumination but problems were found.

Five Hundred Civil Defense Wardens moved about the city telling people to close their blinds, or turn off their lights. One big problem they found were signs that had to be turned off manually. Cigarettes were highly visible from an air plane flying over the city looking for lights. The pilot would call down to the men on the roof by way of two way radio to report lights visible from above. Then word would be passed onto the wardens to respond accordingly.

Nuevo Laredo participated in the air raid drill and did a much better job getting all their lights off quicker than the folks on the east side of the river.

Knowing there was a possibility of communications going down in an emergency, Fort McIntosh began teaching The Boy Scouts to act as runners to deliver messages. The boys would gather at the fort ones a week and then receive instruction on how to maneuver through town during a bombing raid. They were taught how to navigate in the dark since any source of light might attract attention from above. The Scouts were given maps of Laredo and Fort McIntosh with hospitals, government buildings, and all Fire Stations where messages might be sent or received. They also received first aid training. Fearing the Germans might use gas on the area, the Scouts learned how to use gas masks.

A Military Police Battalion was moved to Fort McIntosh under the command of Lt. Colonel John Fletcher and training was begun. As men would arrive for training they needed to be housed and provided for. This led to the building of temporary housing on the south west side of the fort. When the soldiers finished their time in Laredo, they would be sent to whichever location they were assigned to.

The fort also began training soldiers in use of radios for communication. Communicating is a very basic skill but doing so using a two way radio while being shot at can take some getting used to. The Germans had developed advanced direction finders and soldiers had to keep their messages short and to the point.

Not all the training was military. Laredo school teachers were sent to the fort to teach everyone from the lowest private to the general running the place in, everything from math to science.

Many people living in the United States didn't finish school. With a war on, men rushed to join the military putting their education aside. Superintendent Galligan of the Laredo School District began working with the soldiers to give them a better education.

The government built a building on the site of the original Ursuline Convent. The land was sold by the nuns and they moved to a new convent on Corpus Christi Street. Even though the convent was no longer there, the street running north from the building retains the name, Convent Street.

The old convent was torn down in 1941 to make way for the new government building which cost $300,000 to build. In 1943, the building was opened right at the end of the bridge coming from Mexico. The three story building was equipped with a tall tower used by the Border Patrol to keep an eye on the river. The building is still there today, but the Border Patrol doesn't use the tower. Customs Agents use the building for inspections and processing.

Leticia Reyes.

Letty is a student at Laredo College. She was taking classes at the Allied Health Buildings. If you look at these buildings you'll think they look a bit industrial. This is because at one time there were two warehouses at the site of the classrooms. When the warehouses were torn down the buildings that replaced them were built to look the same for historic purposes. The health classrooms are right next to the southern wall of the fort.

As Letty, and one other student were practicing their skills along with the instructor, they all had a feeling there was someone close by. Letty saw someone walk behind them but only momentarily. All they could remember was the person had been wearing boots like a soldier. The rest of the class was in another part of the room and didn't see what was going on.

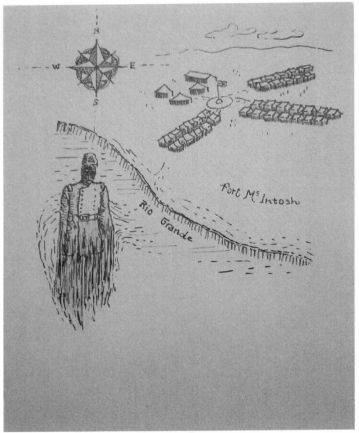

Drawn by Leticia Reyes.

Then, the sound of someone talking was heard. It sounded far away as if from another room. There was a communication window into the next office but that room was dark and there was no one in it. Letty offered to check the store room to see if there was anyone in it but the instructor thought this might be a bad idea. She was frightened of something.

Letty went and opened the door anyway. The room was dark so she turned on the lights. A quick look showed the store room was empty.

There was no explanation as to where the man disappeared to or who was whispering from the back room.

Right where the three had been working used to sit a hospital bed used for student practice. A while ago the bed began to elevate on its own. No one was near the controls. Somehow the peddle that raised the bed was now under one of its wheels.

Letty drew the cover image as well as the inside drawing.

Frank Gonzalez.

Frank worked at the Laredo Children's Museum, located at the far West side of the Laredo Community College. The museum, used to be the Fort Macintosh Chapel, back when the college was a military fort.

He often felt as if someone was watching him, anytime he was there alone. As he moved about the building, he would suddenly look over a shoulder, to see who was watching him, but never saw anyone inside or out.

The building has a basement, which isn't unusual for Laredo. The offices for the museum are located there. When closing up for the night, Frank would have to turn out all the lights in the building, and then make his way through the dark, so he could exit the museum.

One night, as he exited the old chapel and walked across the street to his car, the alarm suddenly went off. He quickly returned to the museum, so he could check to see if anything were amiss, and reset the alarm.

He had to walk through the dark, empty, museum. Moving through the 1940s structure, looking for any reason for the alarm. When nothing appeared to be out of place, he reset the alarm and headed back to his car.

Once at his car, the alarm went off again. Frank went back into the museum, once more checking for the cause of the alarm, and resetting the system so he could leave.

Getting back to his car, he was surprised by the sound of, you guessed it, the alarm going off. He walked back across the street, up the stairs, into the darkened building. A quick check showed no signs of disturbance. As Frank walked back to the exit, the sound of something crashing to the floor near the back of the museum, caught him by surprise. Nothing should have, or could have, made so much noise.

Having had enough, Frank got in his car, and got out of there. The campus police could handle the next alarm, should it go off.

The next day, as he returned to work, Frank asked the day shift if they had found anything in the museum that might have caused all the commotion. They told him there was nothing out of place, and nothing laying on the floor.

Captain Earl Houk proposed the creation of a Base Newspaper that would deal with things going on in the fort. The paper would be a place to write about things of interest to soldiers. The Captain asked for anyone with artistic talent, and a sense of humor, contact him in order to be considered as a contributor to the soon to be newspaper. He placed Pvt. George Stebbins, of the 1860th Service Unit, in charge of the day to day activities of the paper. It was to be called "The Blaze." The paper would come out every other month.

In May, 1942, soldiers from Fort McIntosh were told to assemble at 0830. They were informed that "Enemy troupes had taken over the town of Hebbronville, 58 miles east." This was a practice war game but the men were to precede with all haste.

Captain Little took forty motorcycles and road east. His unit consisted of eighty men armed with sidecar machine guns. They were followed a few minutes later by Captain John with his troupes loaded into trucks.

Within minutes the heavy equipment unit drove out of the fort and headed east. These men carried mortars and antitank rockets.

By 10:00 AM Captain Little and his men road into Hebbronville and took possession of the court house, bank and public office. He then sent word to Captain John giving him a rundown of the size, shape, and layout of the town.

As John's men arrived they were sent to take command of the railroad station and telephone office. The heavy equipment unit set up a perimeter to handle any counter attack.

The folks living in Hebbronville were treated to a display of military might without running the risk of being shot.

Soldiers do have some free time. Not everyone wants to spend their off hours playing pool or baseball. In January 1943 Corporal Teddy Wald announced anyone interested in building models, should come to the Chapel where a model building club was being formed.

A model club was formed and the soldiers could spend their

off hours building airplanes and ships. These models didn't come in a box. The person building either a plane or ship would have a handful of small wood strips and cloth. Each piece had to be cut and glued together forming the shape of whatever you were building. This could take months but the end product was worth it.

In 1943 the air field at Fort McIntosh was too short to support larger planes coming into the field or taking off. 400 feet of Anna Street which was just north of the end of the field was leased from the city and turned into part of the runway. This would allow larger planes to land at Fort McIntosh and the Civil Air Patrol could come and go without interfering with training at the Laredo Army Airfield.

January 19, 1944 the Civil Air Patrol were flying out of the air strip at Fort McIntosh. They would fly the border looking for suspicious activity on either side of the Rio Grande. The war was still on and there was the possibility of enemy soldiers trying to enter the country to wreak havoc on any vital institutions like the railway system or the air fields.

Lt. Harry Hewett from Eugene Oregon, and his partner Bayard Henderson from Blackbird, Delaware were attached to the 56th Cavalry Brigade. They were flying north along the river when their plane crashed twenty miles upriver.

The bodies were returned to their home towns after the inquest.

That same year, training was being conducted in Mirando City, 35 miles east of Laredo. Soldiers from other parts of the country would be sent out to travel the ranches in order to teach them how to navigate in rough terrane. A company from Fort Brown were detailed to Fort McIntosh and then sent east to find objectives and then return.

Private James Horne, 29, from Brownsville, Texas was driving a jeep when he hit an arroyo and the jeep fell sideways. The rest of the training unit rushed to the scene of the accident.

Horne was found dead under the jeep and his companions were in need of medical treatment. The soldiers were rushed to the hospital at Fort McIntosh and Private Horne's body was removed from the arroyo and sent to Laredo. He was shipped home soon after.

In 1944, the Fort McIntosh Adjutant was finding a problem with the live fire rang north of the fort. There was nothing wrong with the range, it was the civilians who would run around on the range when the army wasn't there that were causing a problem.

The range was six miles north of town on the east side of Highway 81. Highway 81 ran north out of town and later became Interstate 35.

People would wander about the range picking up anything of interest. Things like unexploded mortar rounds and faulty hand grenades. What some folks don't know about these killing devices is, once they have been fired, if they didn't explode, they might go off simply because someone stepped on them let alone picked them up.

The Adjutant put out the word for the civilians to stay away from the range and stop taking deadly souvenirs home.

11 THE END FOR FORT MCINTOSH

At the end of World War II, the government began centralizing the military into larger forts located in the interior of the country. It was no longer necessary to maintain border facilities.

The forts built back in the 1800s and early 1900s were returned to the cities that owned the land these forts had been built on. Fort McIntosh was owned by the government but the land belonged to Laredo. Laredo Junior College was created on September 28, 1947, by the Laredo Independent School District in Laredo.

This would allow people living in the community to attend classes to learn technical skills. Things like auto mechanics, electronics, or welding.

The streets on the fort had been named after military leaders but not necessarily the people thought of when seeing the names. Sherman Road was not named for General William Tecumseh Sherman. The road was named for Captain W.C. Sherman, the man who developed the 8th Engineers, Co. A at the fort in 1916.

Sheridan Road was named for P.H. Sheridan, who served as a 2nd Lieutenant of the 1at Infantry at Fort McIntosh in 1854. During the Civil War Sheridan rose through the ranks and soon became General of the Army.

Bee Road is no longer drivable. It ran in front of Arechiga Hall and the other barracks. Captain Hamilton Bee was Captain Lamar's second in command back in 1847 when the first United States troops arrived in Laredo.

General Zachery Taylor was in command of the United States forces during the Mexican-American War. He later went on to become the twelfth president. The road running from Moctezuma past the Army Reserve Center is named for him.

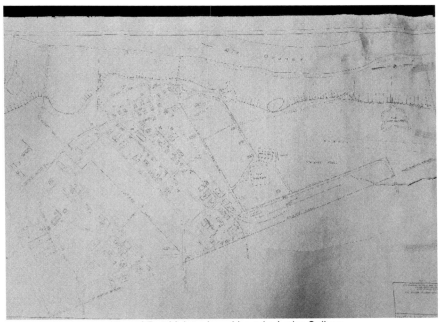

Map of Fort McIntosh and Laredo Junior College
No date could be found on its origination
Image curtesy of Laredo Public Library

Hudson Road was named for Lieutenant Walter Hudson who died from injuries in 1850 while engaged in battle north of the fort. He was the first soldier to die while station at Fort McIntosh.

When the star fort was first built, it was named Camp Crawford. Crawford Road is named for the original star fort which had been named after Secretary of War George W. Crawford.

As the college grew some of the roads were closed and built over. This would allow the college to use the land more wisely. Old building were torn down and new ones were erected.

In 1947, the college adopted the name the "Golden Palominos" and began using green, gold, and white as the school colors.

That year the library was just one room with 4,000 books. The librarian Delia Lynn Westbrook worked hard to get the "reading room" turned into something bigger. She wanted to get the old fort chapel as the library. It was to be named the "Fort McIntosh Memorial Chapel and Library." President Adkins went to San Antonio and spoke with the Chaplin's Association to see if this could be done.

In 1948, the college welcomed their first football team, the Palominos. Coach Bailey "Pappy" Drennan announced the first practice was to be held on September 1st at the new football field. That same year the college formed their first basketball team as well, also called the Palominos.

On February 28, 1950, 19 year old Hector Sandoval decided he wanted to take a trip north. He jumped a north bound train leaving from the Missouri Pacific rail yard. At mile marker 3, north of town he slipped and fell from the train, dying on impact. Hector had been in the military and he was taking classes at Laredo Junior College.

In May, 1950 the school began offering Home Economics classes. Dian Lafon opened the "Homemaking Cottage" where women would learn sowing and cooking. The classes were held five days a week, for two hours each day. The Home Ec classes continued up until 1960 when some changes were made.

The Laredo High School had been in San Agustin Plaza for years. When it was moved the building became the Katherine Tarver School, located on the south side of San Agustin Plaza, right around the corner from the church. In the late 50s, the school was having some problems with students not showing up for class. Many of the students were from migrant farming families or families that worked in the fields. Education wasn't considered to be as important as putting food on the table. The school had been originally set up to handle these kids allowing them to make up classes when they could. The curriculum was designed to teach things beneficial to farming while still helping the kids advance.

In December, 1959, the middle of the school year, the school board met in a closed door session and voted to close the school. They then went on to approve of a plan to sell the land. There was a developing company interested in constructing a hotel near the downtown area. Once the votes had been cast someone asked what they were going to do with the kids.

President Adkins said there was a building on the campus that might fit the bill. He offered the Homemaking Cottage as a school until a new location could be arranged.

The children of the farm workers were moved to Laredo Junior College for their teaching. Later on, land was purchased on Tilden Avenue were the school was finally moved.

Once the Tarver School was torn down the "La Posada Hotel" was built on the land formerly occupied by the school.

The Border Patrol was established in 1924 to stop the influx of immigrants from China. Since most of these folks were coming north by way of Mexico, the first Border Patrol station was built in El Paso, Texas which was approximately the midpoint of the border between San Diego, California and Brownsville, Texas.

United States Border Patrol Station and Headquarters
located in the old hospital at Fort McIntosh.
Image courtesy of the National Border Patrol Museum
In El Paso, Texas

Laredo Sector was established the same year. The station was moved from one location to another until it found its way to Fort McIntosh in 1956. The old hospital was to be used as Headquarters and the station. Since the hospital was built in 1886, maintenance was a constant issue. The wiring had to be checked on a regular basis to prevent fire.

The Border Patrol was awarded 21 acres of land which include the run way, and 19 buildings to be used for airplane storage, and maintenance, vehicle maintenance, equipment storage and radio operations.

The United States Air Corps was leasing one building and they would share the air strip. The Deputy Chief Patrol Inspector was renting one of the residences.

The radio antenna that the United States Army had built back in 1917 was to be used by the Patrol. The radio call sign was KAK-940. At the time the tower was built all radio messages were sent out in Morris Code. When voice able radios came into use, mobile radios were not very powerful so repeater stations were put in around the sector to boost radio signals. KAK-942 was located in Cotulla, north from Laredo. KAK-944 was in Hebbronville.

To keep the agents firearms proficiency up to par, there was a firing range built next to the eastern wall of Fort McIntosh just north of Taylor Road. Today, there is a parking lot where the range used to be located.

A watch tower was built on the river to the west of the station. This tower would give an agent the ability to watch the river for anyone trying to enter illegally.

The Border Patrol began using the air field at Fort McIntosh. There were two planes the patrol used to fly along the river or head inland to help look for groups who had already crossed. They also helped local law enforcement to look for escaped criminals or people who were lost on the ranches and fields around Webb County.

The Border Patrol didn't hire pilots to fly patrols. Anyone wishing to be a BP pilot had to first become an agent. Once they had two years of active duty the agent could apply for training as a pilot. Having a private license was also necessary.

In November, 1961, Noel Williams became the first Border Patrol Agent to be trained at Fort McIntosh Field.

Agents Dale Burt and Leroy Harris had come to Laredo as pilot instructors. They certified Williams as a pilot after he had completed 600 hours of flight time. Part of the training was how to follow tracks from the air, and use a two way radio to contact agents on the ground. Williams also had to know all of the ranches and roads in Webb County so he could pass on the information.

Chief James Kelley issued Williams his wings.

Williams was still required to perform normal patrol duties. When a pilot was called for, he would switch over to the pilot's seat and fly.

The Border Patrol had two airplanes stationed at the fort. A Piper Super Cub, and a Champion Challenger.

That same year, Chief Kelley was host to several officials from South Vietnam. They had come to the fort to see how the United States Border Patrol operated so they could take the information back home.

One item of interest was the BP tower to the west of the station. It was right on the river and had a spot light mounted on the tower so agents could scan the river at night looking for people trying to cross illegally.

The Vietnamese Officials were in Laredo for a few days before departing for another sector.

Senior Patrol Agent Galvan told me, his first duties when he arrived in Laredo in 1962 was to transport boxes and equipment to the new Sector Head Quarters on Del Mar Boulevard.

For years I've heard about a photograph, taken by a Border Patrol Agent who was driving through Laredo College. The photo shows what looked like a woman and four children standing outside one of the old Officers Barracks built in the 1940s. The agent was driving late at night and took the photos of the buildings. At the time there was no one out walking on the campus.

Over the years I have asked agents I know if they had a copy of these photos. People would tell me they'd seen the images but didn't have a copy of them. When I visited the Police Station at Laredo College one of the officers told me he had a copy but was unable to track it down.

I was going to leave the photos out all together when I just happened to mention my search to Ismael Cuellar, the Founder of the LPRS. He told me he not only had seen the images but had them at home. As soon as he was able he sent me copies so I included them here in the book.

The first image shows the east side of the officers dorm. If you look closely you'll see some hazy shapes that look like people to the left of the photo between the signs at the front of the building.

Photo curtesy of Laredo Paranormal Research Society.

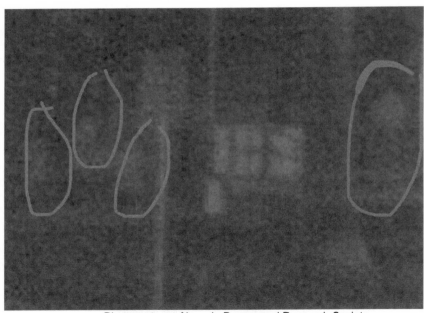

Photo curtesy of Laredo Paranormal Research Society.

The agent didn't see anyone standing in front of the building. He only saw the figures once the images had been developed.

170

On May 14, 1948, just one day before the expiration of the British Mandate governing the area known as Palestine created by the League of Nations in 1923, David Ben-Gurion declared the establishment of a Jewish state in Eretz-Israel to be known as the State of Israel.

If you follow a line running west for 7,000 miles you'll find Texas. The two share the same latitude. Israel consists of 12,877 square miles of land. Texas comes in at 268,596 square miles, 20 times the size.

Israel is a major exporter of fresh produce as well as a world-leader in agricultural technologies and development. This despite the fact that the geography of the country is not naturally conducive to agriculture. More than half of the land area is desert, and the climate and lack of water resources do not favor farming. Yet the Israelis managed to make the desert bloom.

Texas has a similarly diverse climate going from mountains to desert to forest. As farming began to boom in Israel the folks in Texas took notice.

The Texas-Israel Exchange Program was formally established in 1985 through the signing of a Memorandum of Agreement between the governments of Texas and Israel. The memoranda stated that there was considerable potential to work together on projects related to energy, trade, marketing and processing, crop development, water use and conservation, research, and joint ventures.

In 1987, the Texas Israeli Exchange or TIE established its first project in Laredo at Fort McIntosh. The Laredo Junior College had offered 100 acres of land along the Rio Grande for the farm's creation. A feasibility study was financed by the Jewish National Fund, and three Israeli consultants came to layout the plans for the farm. Dr. Juaquin Juarez was involved in the farm project and James Hightower ran things from the state side as Agriculture Secretary. The first crops planted were in the spring of 1988, which included tomatoes, peppers, melons, and specialty cucumbers.

The secret that made the Israelis a success was they ran plastic pipes along the entire field to slowly drip water to the plants and covered the ground around the plants with plastic to hold the moisture in. This generated a high yield crop with very little water.

Buildings were put up to house equipment and produce. These where built using straw bales and mud. To keep the farm buildings cool on hot summer days the structures were all equipped with evaporation cooling towers. This gave the building a very distinct appearance.

The Lamar Bruni Vergara Environmental Science Center.
The two cooling towers give the building a distinct look.

In 1991, the Texas Israel Exchange Board was formally appointed. They focused on more of a transfer of knowledge between Texas and Israeli scientists on improving agricultural and livestock production. The Fort McIntosh farm funding came to an end so the area was proposed to be cleared for a parking lot.

The Rio Grande International Study Group, RGISC, were located on the campus. They asked to "rent" the property for $1 a year to be used to study the river.

RGISC set up tables with aquariums and terrariums to show some of the plants and animals that lived in and along the river. They set out to teach people why it was important to keep the river clean. Volunteers built a trail through the brush so people could walk and enjoy nature (the Paso del Indio Nature and History Trail opening in 1994). Bird watchers began to flock to the area to observe the creatures that used Fort McIntosh as a rest stop while migrating from one area to the next.

Lamar Bruni Vergara, was born in 1910 in Laredo, Texas. She dedicated many hours to the Catholic Church and local social service organizations. Having no children of her own, as she was growing close to the end, she put together a trust fund. Money was to be used for education, health, and religion in Webb County.

When RGISC was incorporated as a nonprofit organization they were able to get $500,000 grant from the Lamar Bruni Vergara Trust. The Laredo Community college matched this amount bringing the total to $1,000,000. This enabled the RGISC to enhance the former Israeli farm.

Tomas (Thomas) Miller, a teacher at J B Alexander, was hired as a temporary director in June or 1999; he took a permanent position as the Director of the Lamar Bruni Vergara Science Center in October.

One project of interest to the center was why there were no alligator in the Rio Grande River. They acquired two American

Alligators from the Gladys Porter Zoo to study and see if there was some environmental reason for the lack of large reptiles along the Rio Grande. The surprising discovery was there are alligators in the river, just few people ever see them.

A group of baby alligators were found in the river near La Bota Ranch just North of Laredo. The babies were rounded up and sent to Nuevo Laredo where a new zoo was established. In 2012 or 13 a seven to eight foot alligator was seen on the banks of the river near El Cenizo. People have also spotted alligator wallows along the brush line near the river.

The next surprise was when one of the alligator gave birth to a batch of babies. Both reptiles were supposed to be females. The babies wound up being eaten by the snapping turtles in the same pit. The remaining alligators died from pneumonia.

Lacking any large reptiles to study, the center was relived to acquire a new batch from Buffalo, New York. A Customs Agent who had been in Laredo but transferred to New York discovered five alligators being brought into the country. The creatures were seized and then shipped to the science center.

As folks began using the nature trails, animals were seen on Fort McIntosh that no one expected to see. A Jaguarundi was seen in 2004. This wild cat is distinct in that it has a small head and very long tail. The tail is as long as the body. In 2011 an Ocelot was seen by Border Patrol Agents working the brush on the fort.

Wild Turkey and Javelina also make their homes in the brush on Fort McIntosh.

The Lamar Bruni Vergara Science Center has an ongoing project to investigate what crops will grow in the Laredo area and which crops need to be shaded using a structure known as a "High Tunnel," that looks like a shady tunnel.

This next story was sent to me by Emily Meza. Here is her story as she gave it to me.

"My boyfriend and I were playing Pokémon Go and he had told me there was a 'stop' at the Cemetery behind the LEAC. When we went down the path towards the memorial, I saw some soldiers, very old-fashioned looking, standing around the cemetery that popped up out of nowhere. They had on green uniforms like the ones used during World War II and I believe there were seven of them. I froze not knowing what I was looking at. My boyfriend said, 'Let's go.' I turned around towards him and then turned back and the soldiers were gone. I ran back to where my boyfriend was and followed him away from the cemetery. After I had told him what I had seen he kept trying to scare me and making fun of me to this day. I don't know if I'm supposed to be scared or amazed."

The LEAC is the Sports Complex at Laredo College.

In 1997 construction was taking place to renovate some of the building being used for the college. A backhoe was digging a trench near the old granary that had been built in 1887. The machine operator didn't know he had hit a gas pipe buried in the ground.

After about two hours the gas had infiltrated the granary and found an ignition source. The building blew up scattering bricks in all directions. The backhoe had moved away from the building and no one was injured but the building was badly damaged. It was a Saturday so few people were around at the time of the explosion.

It was a sad occurrence to an historic site. The granary had been turned into a Tayler shop during World War II and then was used to store tennis equipment. The print shop was built in what was left of the damaged granary.

THE BACK OF THE OLD GRANARY

12 AFTER ALL THAT

Today, the fort is known as Laredo College. It has gone through a few name changes and many reconfigurations. The walls of the original star fort have settled into the ground or been blown away by the wind. The shape can still be seen from above but the fort is in need of restoration.

The ghost investigations and guest tours held in October, 2018 can be described as being way too much in too short of a time period. The idea was sound but the logistics were beyond the LPRSs ability to manage.

It was not the investigations or tours but the total amount of video, audio, and personal experiences that overwhelmed the team's ability to sort out evidence from misidentified objects.

The LPRS held eight nights of tours. There were four to six tours each night. Each group consisted of between six and ten guests. Every person there had recording equipment or photography gear. Memory chips were filled and swapped out. Images and videos were downloaded onto computers for later inspection. There were around 380 hours of audio and thousands of images to be dealt with.

Due to the mass of materials collected over the month, only a small amount was ever reviewed. It takes more time to review than to investigate.

Each tour resulted in many personal experiences. Many of the students and staff at the college told of seeing, smelling, or feeling something unexplainable during their time with the LPRS. The members of the investigations team also reported having unexplained experiences.

It is no wonder the grounds formerly known as Camp Crawford, Fort McIntosh, Laredo Junior College, Laredo Community College and Laredo College holds so many unexplainable events. The energy expended by men stationed at the fort, many of whom wished they were someplace else. The people who died through accidents or murders. We might ask, when a person dies, where does their energy go? If a person is extremely upset, say, sitting in the guardhouse or working in the hot sun, where does the emotion go as it leaves their bodies?

I read as many newspapers from back in the time the fort was used by the military. I could never find any articles dealing with a young girl who died anywhere in the vicinity of the fort. Many of the papers are missing from the archives and the article may just be misplaced. So many people have seen her yet we don't know her name. Maybe someday we can find her name and family history, Until then she will be known only as the Little Girl.

The lady in white is another anomaly. Some folks think she might be the spirit of Ethyl Carlos, the young mother killed by her estranged lover. Others think she might be an English Teacher that used to work at the school neat the south side of the fort.

Soldiers have been seen all around the fort dressed in uniforms from the late 1800s until the end of World War II. Only two men died from wounds received in battle. Many others died from disease, suicide, murder, or accidents. During World War II security was tight and many records were not published in the papers. Several prisoners were shot while attempting to escape. Any of these men could have found reason to linger after their deaths.

During several investigations the name Lt. Karl was recorded. I could never find a record of a Lt. Karl, or Carl serving at Fort McIntosh but thousands of troupes passed through the gates of the fort and not all of them were listed in the records.

Can it be said, Fort McIntosh is haunted? I would say definitely. All of the sightings written up in this book came from either talking directly to the person involved or by someone who knew the witness and vouched for their candor.

There are many more encounters that the folks involved chose to keep to themselves, either out of fear of ridicule, or simply they convinced themselves it never happened.

If you happen to be at Laredo College and you see something you can't explain, send me a note. This book is finished but there could always be another one.

I would like to thank all the folks who helped make this book happen. The people that came forward and told their stories and the people that helped in my research. Without all their help I would never have been able to write this book.

strangethings@arcanasa.com

ABOUT THE AUTHOR

Chris James is a retired Border Patrol Agent. He lives in Laredo, Texas
with his wife, dog Mark, and a bunch of cats. He spends his days
looking into strange things all around town. When he's not researching
a book he's getting ready for his podcast,
"Strange Things with Chris James"
which you can find online at
strangethings.podomatic.com
or on You Tube.

His first nonfiction book is:
"The Laredo Paranormal Research Society."
He has written twenty fiction books.

Chris James

Made in the USA
Columbia, SC
03 September 2020